# Contents

# Jesus sat down

The work is done! King Jesus reigns – and is sitting down at the right hand of the Father (Hebrews 1:3)! So, Ro Willoughby, in her series on Hebrews, helps us to remember the reigning Jesus. As we wrote this, we had just witnessed the passing of Queen Elizabeth II and the accession of King Charles III. In this *Daily Bread*, we will meet many kings of God's people, good and bad (1 Kings 12–22), and there is the central theme of their obedience and faithfulness to God – a lynchpin in their well-being.

Our world with its present wars, rumours of war, famine, natural and economic disasters, idolatry and injustice, doesn't seem so different from the times of the kings and prophets who we will meet in our Bible readings over the coming weeks. As Gethin Russell-Jones reminds us through his series on Isaiah, our God, with eternal perspective, sees the big picture. He watches over his people and knows that those who work evil will be defeated. Meanwhile, day by day, we live in a world where Jesus walked; he understands our everyday experience. Like those earlier disciples, we discover that he is with us in the midst of the storm (Mark 4:35–41, ESV), and our powerful king reassures us: 'Peace! Be still!'

In these changing times, we need to remember that it is King Jesus who reigns. Sin and evil *are* defeated, our sin is forgiven, injustices will be put right. Resurrection and the renewing of God's creation are a present-future certainty, and: 'Your throne, O God, will last for ever and ever' (Hebrews 1:8).

**'Tricia and Emlyn Williams**
Editors

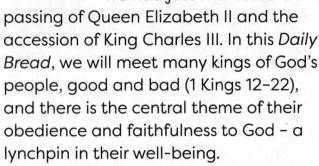

# Daily Bread toolbox

**Tricia & Emlyn Williams** worked with Scripture Union for many years. Emlyn led Schools ministry, then worked with SU International. Tricia was also part of the Schools team and later worked for SU Publishing, developing, writing and editing Bible resources. Having recently completed research in the area of faith and dementia, she continues with writing and editing faith resources. Retired from his role as discipleship pastor in a local church, Emlyn now continues his writing and talking-with-people ministries.

## WAY IN

This page introduces both the notes and the writer. It sets the scene and tells you what you need to know to get into each series.

## A DAY'S NOTE

The notes for each day include five key elements: *Prepare, Read* (the Bible passage for the day), *Explore, Respond* and *Bible in a year.* These are intended to provide a helpful way of meeting God in his Word.

## PREPARE

Prepare yourself to meet with God and pray that the Holy Spirit will help you to understand and respond to what you read.

## READ

Read the Bible passage, taking time to absorb and simply enjoy it. A verse or two from the Bible text is usually included on each page, but it's important to read the whole passage.

## EXPLORE

Explore the meaning of the passage, listening for what God may be saying to you. Before you read the comment, ask yourself: what is the main point of this passage? What is God showing me about himself or about my life? Is there a promise or a command, a warning or example to take special notice of?

## RESPOND

Respond to what God has shown you in the passage in worship and pray for yourself and others. Decide how to share your discoveries with others.

## BIBLE IN A YEAR

If your aim is to know God and his Word more deeply, why not follow this plan and read the whole Bible in one year?

# The God of surprises

In under a year, Fiona Beck has become a children's and families' worker and Faith Guide, and has established an incredibly popular after-school club. She has set her sights and prayers on it becoming a Grow Community. The first green shoots of faith are already appearing.

Fiona has a long history with Scripture Union. She became a Christian on an SU camp in Scotland, became a leader at 17 and later started volunteering regularly at Port St Mary Beach Mission, where she met her husband. Sarah Howard-Smith, SU North Support Worker, visited the Beach Mission in the summer of 2021 and shared the Revealing Jesus mission framework and about being a Faith Guide. 'I thought it was a great idea,' Fiona says, 'but at the time I felt it wasn't for me.

'God of course knew different! Before I went home, a godly couple prayed with me and I felt led to look at a

Christian jobs website. I saw that St Andrew's Church in Cheadle Hulme (near my home) was looking for a children's worker. I'd been working in a supermarket, although it was my volunteering with church and with SU that defined me. So I applied for the church role and, to my amazement, I got the job. I never saw that coming! Now I had every reason to be a Faith Guide, so I signed up, did my training and began planning what to do next.'

## Wonderful church support

Over a number of years, the church had lost the few families it had, so they were very keen to reach out to children and young people in the wider community. They were so keen, in fact, that 35 of the 50 congregation members volunteered to help Fiona. 'I only work 20 hours a week,' Fiona says, 'so I have felt really blessed by their support. I try to align the roles with what they like doing and are good at. So far it's worked!'

## Making connections with families

SU's Revealing Jesus mission framework incorporates four stages: Connect, Explore, Respond and Grow. Within weeks of starting in her new role in September, Fiona and her team of volunteers began to connect with local children and their families. 'We organised a Light Party using SU materials to create a Light Trail,' says Fiona. 'In the best tradition, it poured with rain, everyone got wet and we all had to come inside! But we got chatting to parents over refreshments

and it started to get me known in the community.'

## '... the next week 51 turned up and soon we had to start a waiting list ...'

Fiona was already looking ahead to the next stages of the faith journey with plans to launch an after-school club, K@STA (Kasta, or Kids@St Andrews), in the January. 'Meantime, we continued to build up connections with children and families,' she says. 'I took on the running of the parents and tots groups which has around 70 members in all. We also put on other events, connected with local schools and promoted K@STA on social media. We prayed and left it in God's hands.'

## 'God's been so good to us'

Fiona was astonished when 29 children arrived for the first K@STA session! She says, 'Word must have gone around the playground because the next week 51 turned up and soon we had to start a waiting list. By the time we broke up for summer, over 130 children, mostly from non-Christian homes, had attended the club since it began seven months earlier. Not all come to every session – the average weekly attendance is around 50. God's been so good to us, we've never had an unmanageable number.

'It's amazing to think that the number of children at the club each week matches the number of people in the entire church congregation!'

# SU article

**Friday night fun**

K@STA takes place on a Friday night. Fiona says, 'We have three groups in different rooms. For the first half hour it's free time and they can do whatever activities they fancy. We have football or another organised game for the active ones, board games in another room and a quieter craft room where children can just hang out and chat. That's something we introduced in response to a request from some of the older children. We were so busy keeping them busy that they said there wasn't enough time to sit and ask the leaders questions about things that were on their minds!

'Then we go through to the church. We sing a couple of songs, with an activity in between. For the first half term we had "twenty questions" with the leaders. There were some fun questions involved, to help engage the quieter children, but also more serious questions around why they believe in God. The next half term, we used some short animation videos where Jesus comes on and talks about a particular theme from the Gospels. Then the final term we evolved the teaching once more and started asking three questions about the video for them to discuss with a leader in small friendship groups.

'Towards the end of the summer term, we opted to go back to free play again after refreshments, hoping that some of the children would engage with the leaders about the Bible story they had just heard.'

**Journeys towards faith**

One local mum has seven children. Fiona says, 'She brought her youngest to the parents and tots group. I got chatting with her and it turned out that she had six other children. I told her about K@STA and she said that she was sure they would love to come to the club. But she was worried too, as one child is thought to have autism. We talked it through and I said, "Well let's have a go and see how it works out," and actually it's been great.'

'... we really began to see a positive change in their behaviour ...'

When Fiona and SU Mission Enabler Sarah Davison ran a *Diary of a Disciple Holiday Club* at Easter, those children came to that as well. Then the oldest three went to SU's Edale Holiday with Fiona. 'Initially they bickered,' she recalls, 'but we really began to see a positive change in their behaviour. Their mum has started putting prayer requests into our prayer box at church, so I hope she is on the journey towards faith too!'

Perhaps the most exciting development is one five-year-old saying to her mum that she wanted to become a Christian after just a few weeks at K@STA. 'Her mum came to me and said, "What does that even mean, being a Christian?" So I told her more about what we believe and prayed with her daughter, who now wants to be baptised. I can't say I saw that coming, either!

'During this adventure, God has shown that he is truly full of delightful surprises. I wonder what the next one will be!'

A shorter version of this story first appeared in *Connecting You*, Scripture Union's free quarterly supporter magazine. If you'd like to receive copies of *Connecting You* and learn more of how God is moving in the hearts and lives of children and young people today, you can sign up on our website at su.org.uk/connectingyou.

# Growth against the odds

These chapters describe the early church growing in the face of opposition. It was an exciting but challenging time. The persecution recorded at the start of our readings took place shortly after Jesus' death and resurrection (probably around AD 33). Paul's meeting with the risen Jesus likely took place in AD 34. Dates after that are difficult to identify until the death of Herod in AD 44. (This is not Herod the Great who killed the babies in Bethlehem, nor Herod Antipas who ruled Galilee during the time of Jesus' ministry, but Herod Agrippa, Herod the Great's grandson.) This suggests that the execution of James and the imprisonment of Peter took place in AD 43.

Luke selects his material carefully, concentrating on specific episodes. He emphasises the powerful activity of God through the Holy Spirit. He shows ordinary people telling others about Jesus. He demonstrates that the good news of Jesus was for all people – Jews and non-Jews. To us this may not seem a big issue, but it was a key truth that the early church struggled to learn. There is an honesty in the way he recounts the events; the early Christians have weaknesses but are still used by God.

Despite the differences in our context and circumstances, there is much that we can learn from these chapters. Be encouraged by the way that God's power is displayed through his people. Be challenged by the welcome that God offers to all. Believe that God is still building his church.

---

About the writer
**John Grayston**

Now retired after 37 years on the Scripture Union staff, John still writes, teaches and preaches. He is on the leadership team at Tile Kiln Church in Chelmsford. When he can he escapes to his allotment, or the mountains walking or skiing with his wife Jenny. He has two children and seven grandchildren.

# God has the last word

## PREPARE
**Pray that you may see things from God's perspective.**

................................................................

## READ
Acts 12:19b–24

## EXPLORE

Tyrants in any age exercise their power in similar ways: violence, as we saw yesterday; or the control of vital supplies – in this case food. In the end, most oppressors overreach themselves. Excessive pride and arrogance become the source of their downfall. Here it is seen in theological terms. Herod receives the adulation of the people, usurps the place of God, and God steps in. The downfall of any oppressor has similar logic. God is the ruler of the nations, the King of kings. He has the ultimate authority, and he will have the last word. We may not see it now. We may, like the saints in Revelation 6:10, cry out, 'How long, Sovereign Lord?' But we can be confident that the time will come when God will reign in justice.

As we struggle with the tension of knowing that God has won the final victory, but that we do not yet see it completely, we can be encouraged by these verses. The Word of God continued to spread. Many of us may live in places where we feel that the church is in decline and may be discouraged. Even there we can find signs of hope, and if we look at the world situation we shall find even more reason to see that, now as then, God's purposes will be accomplished.

> But the word of God continued to spread and flourish.
>
> **Acts 12:24**

## RESPOND
Commit your situation and that of your church to God in the knowledge that he has a plan.

................................................................

**Bible in a year:** 2 Chronicles 33,34; Psalms 75,76

## Sunday 2 July
Psalm 99

# The Lord reigns

## PREPARE
Acknowledge God as the King of your life. Ask him to reveal more of what that might mean in practice.

...............................................................................................................

## READ
**Psalm 99**

## EXPLORE
This psalm might be a comment on yesterday's reading. The Lord reigns, not Herod, nor any other human ruler. The rulers of the nations have power, but only in so far as God allows. The psalm is a celebration of God's rule over Israel. At her best, Israel recognised and lived under God's rule in a way that other nations did not. They thus became, in fulfilment of God's promise to Abraham, a blessing to other nations by modelling what living under God's rule could be like (Genesis 12:2,3). Look back through the psalm to see what marks God's rule.

God is great, awesome and holy – beyond our understanding and yet intimately involved with us. Not only does God rule justly (v 4), he also enters into a relationship with his people. He speaks to them (v 7), he sets boundaries for their own good and he holds them accountable (v 8). The same is true for us as we enter into relationship with

him through Jesus. Israel experienced the forgiveness of God (v 8) through the system of sacrifices, but we find forgiveness through the death of Jesus. So we can join in this wonderful celebration, praising this great God whom we can never fully understand but who is worthy of our worship.

Exalt the LORD our God and worship at his holy mountain, for the LORD our God is holy.
**Psalm 99:9**

---

## RESPOND
Identify three things, from the psalm or from your own experience, for which to praise God – and do it.

---

...............................................................................................................

**Bible in a year:** 2 Chronicles 35,36;  Luke 1:39–80

# Isaiah opens up

About the writer
**Roger Combes**

Roger has ministered in London, Cambridge and East and West Sussex. He and his wife live in Crawley, near Gatwick airport and glorious countryside. Being retired means he can now watch more sport of all kinds. He has supported Bournemouth football club for 60 years.

I'd like to meet Isaiah. As we read his book, Isaiah begins to open up to us as a person. He lived in Jerusalem with his wife and two boys. One wonders whether anyone in the city knew more about what was going on than he did. He moved with ease among kings. He was familiar with everything happening in the Temple. He speaks of the judges and legislators, the elders and the leaders, the snobs and the fashionistas, the poor and the deprived. He fumes at the exploitation of the oppressed and how no one cared or spoke up for them. He was also well informed about world affairs. He gave statesmanlike counsel on foreign policy, though often in vain. He was a passionate and intelligent spokesman for the Lord.

He is also famous as the evangelist of the Old Testament, opening up to us the gospel of God, salvation for the world. The language is always vivid and rich, full of pictures and metaphor. Chapter after chapter is an inspiring call to repent and grasp the hope and redemption of God. Sometimes tender, sometimes blistering, the prophet challenges the people about their lives and behaviour. What does the Lord expect from his people? Faith without hypocrisy, justice without favouritism, righteousness in how we treat other people, and compassion for any in need.

Isaiah prophesied from about 740 to 701 BC. Supremely, he 'saw the Lord'. May we see him too.

# Monday 3 July
## Isaiah 1:1–20

# Hear the Word of the Lord

## PREPARE

**Pray: Lord, please speak to me from your Word. Help me to grasp its practical implications for me, for Christ's sake. Amen.**

. . . . . . . . . . . . . . . . . . . . . . . . . . . . . . . . . . . . . . . . . . . . . . . . . . . . . . . . . . . . . . . . . . . . . .

## READ
### Isaiah 1:1–20

## EXPLORE

When the band strikes up the overture to a musical, we get a taste of what is to come. The main song-tunes are introduced. The early verses of Isaiah do the same. They give us the main themes of Isaiah's message, and perhaps of the Old Testament prophets generally.

*Theme 1.* We need to listen. It is not just Isaiah speaking, but the Lord himself (vs 2,10,20b).

*Theme 2.* Religion without morality is meaningless and abhorrent. Let's not fool ourselves. Church involvement by itself is no proof of goodness. Isaiah was addressing people whose religious attendance every Sabbath was impeccable. They gave sacrificially and prayed continually. They took part in everything (vs 11–15). But their hearts were disloyal and hostile to the Lord (vs 4–6).

*Theme 3.* Change is required. Their everyday behaviour was wrong.

Injustice and corruption continued apace. The marginalised suffered and the economically weak were exploited (vs 16,17). The late Bishop John B Taylor wrote, 'Every Christian should be both a good neighbour and a social reformer.'*

*Theme 4.* The gospel according to Isaiah. Though our sins are startling red, all stain of them shall be removed. The Lord proposes a good future... if we will receive it obediently and not resist him. We have to choose (vs 18–20).

> 'Learn to do right; seek justice. Defend the oppressed. Take up the cause of the fatherless; plead the case of the widow.'
>
> **Isaiah 1:17**

---

### RESPOND
'Holy Lord, thank you that you cleanse us from all sin through Jesus Christ our Saviour. Amen.'

---

*John B Taylor, *Preaching through the Prophets*, Mowbray, 1983, p3

. . . . . . . . . . . . . . . . . . . . . . . . . . . . . . . . . . . . . . . . . . . . . . . . . . . . . . . . . . . . . . . . . . . . . .

**Bible in a year:** Ezra 1,2;  Luke 2

# Redeemer and judge

## PREPARE
Let's begin by giving thanks for all good gifts around us.

. . . . . . . . . . . . . . . . . . . . . . . . . . . . . . . . . . . . . . . . . . . . . . . . .

## READ
**Isaiah 1:21–31**

## EXPLORE
Sometimes a pollster announces that such and such a place has emerged as the most desirable town/village/city to live in. Isaiah used to think of Jerusalem like that. People were trustworthy and did what was right, and there was fairness for all. But now its leaders had jettisoned all this. They were corrupt, grabbing what they could. Anyone with gifts was welcomed, while those with needs (like an orphan or a widow) were dismissed (vs 21–23). Are you not outraged when you hear of someone ill-treating a child or some other defenceless person? So how will the Lord, the Mighty One of Israel, react? He is outraged too, of course, and will judge those who rebel against him by ill-treating the weak (vs 24,28–31). (The 'sacred oaks' and 'gardens' (v 29) were where pagan fertility rites took place. They underline how far Jerusalem had forsaken God's ways.)

But the Lord is not just a judge. He is a redeemer as well. He will restore the city. He knows what it needs: good people to lead, for a start. Although there are many different systems of government, there is no system that is so good that it doesn't need good people! It will need citizens of integrity, who will act well in the nitty-gritty of life. And it will need repentance for the past (vs 25b–27).

## Zion will be delivered with justice, her penitent ones with righteousness.
**Isaiah 1:27**

## RESPOND
The 'fatherless' and the 'widow' (vs 17,23b) had little financial security or support from society in those days. Who are their equivalents needing help today?

. . . . . . . . . . . . . . . . . . . . . . . . . . . . . . . . . . . . . . . . . . . . . . . . .

**Bible in a year:** Ezra 3,4;  Luke 3

# Wednesday 5 July

Isaiah 2:1–22

# What the seer saw

## PREPARE

**The Bible has a remarkable way of giving us a God's-eye view. May we see as he sees.**

••••••••••••••••••••••••••••••••••••••••••••••••••••••••••••••••••••••••••••••••

## READ

**Isaiah 2:1–22**

## EXPLORE

A friend once told me that his parents realised he needed glasses when he couldn't see a battleship that had sailed into the harbour! In this chapter, Isaiah has clear sight of a glorious future, as well as the unedifying present. What the prophet could see embraced 'the last days' and his own day, the heavenly Jerusalem and his own Jerusalem, peoples of the world and the locals.

What will it be like at the end of time? Isaiah gives one of the Bible's earliest answers. He sees the world's peoples streaming to the mountain of the exalted Lord to adopt his way (vs 2–4). He sees that Jerusalem and the world are key in God's plan of salvation. One day, as we know, his Word would go out worldwide (v 3c) from a green hill and an upper room in this Jerusalem. Ultimately, the Lord will reign over a new, re-ordered world. War and armaments will be obsolete (v 4).

By contrast, Isaiah saw that his contemporaries' faith was full of pagan practices, materialism, idolatry and pride (vs 6–18). They must be rejected. God's judgement will be like a violent earthquake from which people will flee (vs 12–21). 'Come … let us walk in the light of the Lᴏʀᴅ' (v 5).

He will judge between the nations … They will beat their swords into ploughshares and their spears into pruning hooks …

**Isaiah 2:4**

## RESPOND

'Lord Jesus, "your kingdom come, your will be done, on earth as it is in heaven" (Matthew 6:10). May my values match the values of heaven. Amen.'

••••••••••••••••••••••••••••••••••••••••••••••••••••••••••••••••••••••••••••••••

**Bible in a year:** Ezra 5,6; Psalm 77

# Shame and the city

## PREPARE
Ask the Lord to show you what you need to know today about him, about yourself and about those your life will touch.

. . . . . . . . . . . . . . . . . . . . . . . . . . . . . . . . . . . . . . . . . . . . . . . . . . . . . . . . . . . . . . . . . .

## READ
Isaiah 3:1 – 4:1

## EXPLORE
The English nursery rhyme 'Mary, Mary, Quite Contrary' does not tell us why Mary was contrary! Some people just enjoy being contrary. They like trying to run up the down escalator, or taking the opposite view in a discussion.

In Isaiah's Jerusalem, it was infinitely more serious. Instead of loving God, they were defying him (v 8); instead of loving their neighbour, they were crushing the poor (v 15). So Isaiah delivered God's judgement on the city, described in terms of the city being captured (similar to what actually happened when the Babylonians eventually destroyed Jerusalem after Isaiah's death). The Lord will withdraw his support. The people will have no food, no water (v 1), no one capable of leadership (vs 2–7) and no dignity (3:15 – 4:1). They will turn on each other and the city will be flattened (vs 5,6). They will lose everything, like the poor they exploited. Their shame will be complete. As captives, they may even be paraded unwashed, bound, branded and shaven-headed (v 24). Prized possessions and haughty appearance will count for nothing (vs 18–23). Our status symbols can become our condemnation.

Is there any hope? Yes, as we shall see tomorrow. The righteous will reap their reward (v 10). A 'remnant' will survive.

'What do you mean by crushing my people and grinding the faces of the poor?' declares the LORD, the LORD Almighty.

**Isaiah 3:15**

## RESPOND
The Lord knows what poor and powerless people must cope with, but do we? How we act towards them is a key question when the Lord assesses us (v 15).

. . . . . . . . . . . . . . . . . . . . . . . . . . . . . . . . . . . . . . . . . . . . . . . . . . . . . . . . . . . . . . . . . .

**Bible in a year:** Ezra 7,8;  Luke 4

## Friday 7 July
### Isaiah 4:2–6

# The eternal city

## PREPARE
**May reading God's Word humble us and then lift us up.**

. . . . . . . . . . . . . . . . . . . . . . . . . . . . . . . . . . . . . . . . . . . . . . . . . . . . . . . . . . . .

## READ
**Isaiah 4:2–6**

## EXPLORE

Is there a date in your diary that you are anxious about, worried it might bring troubling news? In our earlier readings the Lord referred to a particular day in his diary (eg 2:11,12). He kept repeating this phrase: 'in that day' – a day when the people will face judgement. So when today's passage begins with the words 'in that day' (v 2), we have a sense we know what is coming. But we are surprised. It is wonderful!

A new Jerusalem beckons (vs 3–6). In the midst, all eyes are on the 'Branch of the LORD' (v 2), surely the Lord's Messiah (as later in Jeremiah 23:5,6), the pride and joy of Judah, beautiful and glorious. All is now holy, even the people. These survivors are washed and cleansed, and their names recorded. The Lord God is leading and protecting his people in this, his new creation. Glory and salvation stretch over the scene.

When life is grim, we need something to look forward to. What could be better than a future like this? Isaiah knew that his people, humbled and disgraced, needed a lift. In good times and bad, looking ahead to what 'God has prepared for those who love him' (1 Corinthians 2:9) can be just the incentive and motivation we need.

I saw the Holy City, the new Jerusalem, coming down out of heaven from God, prepared as a bride beautifully dressed for her husband.

**Revelation 21:2**

## RESPOND
Pray: Heavenly Father, thank you that the Lord Jesus endured so much 'for the joy that was set before him' (Hebrews 12:2). Help me to do the same. Amen.

. . . . . . . . . . . . . . . . . . . . . . . . . . . . . . . . . . . . . . . . . . . . . . . . . . . . . . . . . . . .

**Bible in a year:** Ezra 9,10;  Luke 5

# Good vineyard, bad grapes

## PREPARE
Pray: Lord, may your Word penetrate my defences, and bring life and strength to my inner being. Amen.

. . . . . . . . . . . . . . . . . . . . . . . . . . . . . . . . . . . . . . . . . . . . . . . . . . . . . . . . . . . . . . . .

## READ
Isaiah 5:1–7

## EXPLORE
Everyone likes a good song. Isaiah, like any preacher, needs to get the people's attention. So he sings a song. Perhaps it is festival time and crowds are milling about, enjoying the harvest wine and songs.

Isaiah's song is a parable about a much-loved friend who owns a vineyard (vs 1,7a). The vineyard owner (the Lord Almighty) values his vineyard (his people) greatly and goes to great trouble to ensure their security, fruitfulness, growth and development. But when he comes to taste the grape, he spits it out. It is bitter and useless (vs 1,2). The owner is so disheartened that he consigns the vineyard back to waste ground, reversing all the measures he took earlier.

Isaiah's song shows us a God who is both delighted and disappointed (v 7). He delights in us as his people, and he lavishes care on us. Nothing is too much trouble. He is disappointed when we pay him back with a world of bloodshed and the cries of the poor. He is looking for good fruit, which – in this context – is a people who will live the life of righteousness and treat all people fairly (v 7).

'This is to my Father's glory, that you bear much fruit, showing yourselves to be my disciples.'
**John 15:8**

## RESPOND
Are we too predictable in our methods sometimes? If Isaiah used song and Jeremiah used drama, let's encourage the development of everyone's artistic, creative and tech abilities to help express God's truth to the world.

. . . . . . . . . . . . . . . . . . . . . . . . . . . . . . . . . . . . . . . . . . . . . . . . . . . . . . . . . . . . . . . .

**Bible in a year:** Nehemiah 1,2;  Psalm 78:1–37

## Sunday 9 July
Psalm 100

# Jubilate, everybody!

## PREPARE
**Pray: Thank you, Lord Jesus, for opening a way for us into your Father's house, so that we can enter with joy and forgiveness. Amen.**

........................................................................................

## READ
**Psalm 100**

## EXPLORE
This refreshingly direct psalm calls us to rejoice in the Lord, and reminds us why we gladly give him thanks and praise. ('Jubilate', the psalm's old title, simply means 'rejoice'.)

First, the Lord is global. The whole world is summoned to join in (v 1). Secondly, the Lord is good news. He touches our emotions deeply and happily. He generates joy, gladness and singing (v 2). Thirdly, the Lord is God (v 3), sovereign in the affairs of heaven and earth. Just as he fashioned Israel to be his people, so we too belong to him, and he is our shepherd. Fourthly, the Lord is for ever (v 5). His goodness is a constant, and his loving commitment to us is unshakeable. He will prove true to us to the end of time. There is so much to praise him for.

Both praise and thanks are necessary in healthy human relationships. It is all too easy to praise someone, say for good work or a special kindness, but omit to thank them. In view of what we know of the Lord's sovereignty and kindness, the psalmist insists that we make a point of praising and thanking him (twice in verse 4). May our devotion to the Lord be like the psalmist's – joyful and grateful.

> Enter his gates with thanksgiving and his courts with praise; give thanks to him and praise his name.

**Psalm 100:4**

## RESPOND
As part of your worship today, make a point of thanking the Lord for something specific, and rejoice!

........................................................................................

**Bible in a year:** Nehemiah 3,4; Luke 6

# Trouble ahead

## PREPARE
'For the LORD takes delight in his people' (Psalm 149:4). Give thanks to him now for this.

∙∙∙∙∙∙∙∙∙∙∙∙∙∙∙∙∙∙∙∙∙∙∙∙∙∙∙∙∙∙∙∙∙∙∙∙∙∙∙∙∙∙∙∙∙∙∙∙∙∙∙∙∙∙∙∙∙∙∙∙

## READ
Isaiah 5:8–30

## EXPLORE
'Blue flag' beaches mean happy family holidays, safe swimming and clean water. But some beaches display red flags, warning of dangerous tides, swift currents and even, in some places, sharks. Only a fool ignores a red flag. The consequences can be grim.

There are six red flags or 'woes' in this passage. These are a warning to those who live rejecting the Law of the Lord (v 24). They bemoan the sad consequences for them and for their society. Land-grabbers will find their investments are antisocial and strangely unsatisfying (vs 8–10). Excessive drinkers and revellers will find life slipping away (vs 11–15). Those who perversely call right wrong and wrong right, truth a lie and lies the truth (v 20); those who don't consider that they might be wrong (v 21); those who distort justice for some benefit to themselves (vs 22,23) – woe to you! says Isaiah. As the song says, 'There will be trouble ahead.'

Isaiah flags it up for Jerusalem. They will see home life and society disintegrate (eg vs 13,14). The God of Israel, who is the God of history, will act decisively in the coming years (vs 25–30). Is there really 'no one to rescue' (v 29)? It is foolish to spurn the Word and work of God (vs 24,12b).

> Woe to those who call evil good and good evil, who put darkness for light and light for darkness, who put bitter for sweet and sweet for bitter.
>
> **Isaiah 5:20**

## RESPOND
Pray: Gracious Lord, may I receive your Word when you are rebuking me as willingly as when you are encouraging me. Amen.

∙∙∙∙∙∙∙∙∙∙∙∙∙∙∙∙∙∙∙∙∙∙∙∙∙∙∙∙∙∙∙∙∙∙∙∙∙∙∙∙∙∙∙∙∙∙∙∙∙∙∙∙∙∙∙∙∙∙∙∙

**Bible in a year:** Nehemiah 5,6;  Luke 7

## Tuesday 11 July
Isaiah 6:1–13

# I saw the Lord

## PREPARE
Prepare to meet your wonderful God!

. . . . . . . . . . . . . . . . . . . . . . . . . . . . . . . . . . . . . . . . . . . .

## READ
**Isaiah 6:1–13**

## EXPLORE
Meeting someone face to face can be life-changing. It was for Saul on the Damascus road (Acts 9:1–6) and it also was for Isaiah. 'I saw the LORD,' he said, 'My eyes have seen the King, the LORD Almighty' (vs 1,5). It was the most formative experience of his life.

Isaiah was stunned facing the majesty and holiness of God, whose glory filled the earth and whose smoke filled the Temple (vs 1–4). Heavenly beings covered their faces. Isaiah lost all sense of respectability before the One who is 'holy, holy, holy'. 'My God, how wonderful you are, your majesty how bright ... your endless wisdom, boundless power, and awesome purity!'*

'Woe to me! ... I am ruined' (v 5) is Isaiah's reaction, but then he discovers that the Lord in all his holiness is not aloof. The Lord reaches down and takes away the prophet's guilt and cleanses his lips (v 6,7). Immediately, it seems, the prophet is eager to serve. He offers himself (v 8), not knowing what awaits him. Perhaps the ability God looks for most is our avail-ability. Isaiah, foremost among the prophets, is given a hard task. He is to go to this people whose mindset will not receive the message (vs 9,10). So he does this, faithfully and imaginatively, for 40 years amid national disintegration... and a promise of hope (vs 11–13).

Then I heard the voice of the Lord saying, 'Whom shall I send? And who will go for us?' And I said, 'Here am I. Send me!'

**Isaiah 6:8**

## RESPOND
Almighty or all-matey? How similar is our attitude to Isaiah's? In our easy-going age, how should we approach the Holy One, high and exalted, seated on his throne?

*FW Faber (1814–1863)

. . . . . . . . . . . . . . . . . . . . . . . . . . . . . . . . . . . . . . . . . . . .

**Bible in a year:** Nehemiah 7,8;  Luke 8

# Immanuel – God with us

## PREPARE

**Give thanks for those who have prayed for you and strengthened your faith in days past.**

. . . . . . . . . . . . . . . . . . . . . . . . . . . . . . . . . . . . . . . . . . . . . . . . . . . . . . . . . . . . . . . . .

## READ

**Isaiah 7:1–25**

## EXPLORE

Ahaz, king of Judah, wasn't an easy person to help, but he was worried (vs 1,2). It looked as though the northern kingdom of Israel, in league with Aram (Syria), would overrun Judah and Jerusalem (see 2 Kings 16:1–5). Isaiah tried to allay Ahaz's fears and strengthen his faith. When they met, Isaiah brought the Lord's assurance that these neighbouring countries, with their weak leaders, were not as dangerous as they seemed (vs 3–9).

Then the Lord gave the king a sign of hope, showing that the confidence of the people would recover in a few months. For example, a young mother would name her newborn son 'Immanuel', which means 'God with us' (v 14). This sign of hope among the people was also a sign to the king to take the Lord's side. He really needed to, as a far bigger threat, from the mighty Assyria, would arrive before long (vs 17–23).

The early church realised (Matthew 1:23) that the name 'Immanuel', 'God with us', beautifully sums up the person of Christ. God was in Christ, bringing hope to the world. 'God with us' is the humble confidence we have in Christ as we go about our daily life: in school, at home, at work, in trouble and in joy.

'If you do not stand firm in your faith, you will not stand at all.'

**Isaiah 7:9**

## RESPOND

An 'Immanuel' prayer – 'May God be with us/me/you/them' – is good to pray for any occasion or activity. Pray that God will be present to enrich and guide your endeavours and relationships this week.

. . . . . . . . . . . . . . . . . . . . . . . . . . . . . . . . . . . . . . . . . . . . . . . . . . . . . . . . . . . . . . . . .

**Bible in a year:** Nehemiah 9,10;  Psalm 78:38–72

# Maher-Shalal-Hash-Baz!

## PREPARE
'Do not fear, for I am with you' (Isaiah 41:10). The Lord expects his presence to reduce your fear. Do *you*?

## READ
**Isaiah 8:1–18**

## EXPLORE
Some friends of mine named their cat Maher-Shalal-Hash-Baz ('Hash-Baz' for short) because it meant 'quick to the plunder, swift to the spoil' (v 1). A dangerous predator for Isaiah's Jerusalem was the kingdom of Assyria, which would soon invade and plunder Judah's northern enemies. The Lord told Isaiah and his wife to name their new son Maher-Shalal-Hash-Baz, as a living sign to the people of Judah that they too would be pounced on, overwhelmed and plundered (vs 7,8).

The Lord then encourages his prophet. Don't live in dread of disaster, of conspiracies or rumours (v 12). The nations of the world may launch unspeakably wicked wars, and they may or may not prosper. But God remains; he is still with us – Immanuel (vs 8,10). Fearsome as the threat may be, the Lord Almighty is the one to trust and fear, more than a powerful enemy, though this will be too much for some to swallow. It would be their downfall (vs 13–15).

The people were unresponsive, and the Lord was 'hiding' from them. So Isaiah withdrew a little to reinforce God's instruction to his disciples. Isaiah himself would take the opportunity to renew his own trust in the Lord, and wait (vs 16,17).

I will wait for the LORD, who is hiding his face from the descendants of Jacob. I will put my trust in him.

**Isaiah 8:17**

## RESPOND
Are you more inclined to exaggerate threats and problems or to be in denial of them? Perhaps Immanuel, God being with you, can help you bring them into a truer perspective.

**Bible in a year:** Nehemiah 11,12; Luke 9

# The Prince of Peace

## PREPARE
**They say night is darkest just before the dawn. That may not be true, but it reminds us not to give up. Seek hope today in Jesus, 'the true light' (John 1:9).**

. . . . . . . . . . . . . . . . . . . . . . . . . . . . . . . . . . . . . . . . . . . . . . . . . . . .

## READ
**Isaiah 8:19 – 9:7**

## EXPLORE

A prom ball after exams. A wrap party after filming. A feast when the harvest is gathered in. All these customary celebrations mark the successful end of a time of intense pressure and effort. Relax! It's over!

One day we shall really celebrate. Isaiah tells us why (9:3–6). Despite all the gloomy warnings and judgements to fall on God's people living in darkness, one day it will be over. The Lord will have won them a victory even better than the great victories of their history. The blows of judgement from various invading armies will have ceased. The light will shine. This is all because of someone unique, given four majestic titles here. Of all the prophecies of the Messiah pointing to the Lord Jesus, verse 6 (which we hear every Christmas) is surely one of the greatest.

Which of these names (v 6) means most to you? *Wonderful Counsellor* – an extraordinary friend. *Mighty* for every need, and *God*, no less. *Everlasting Father* – father par excellence and father of eternity. *Prince of Peace* – a prince unlike any other, at one with God and at peace with himself, whose reign will be one of peace and harmony, justice and righteousness, well-being and fulfilment, for ever (v 7). We may start rejoicing now.

For to us a child is born, to us a son is given … And he will be called Wonderful Counsellor, Mighty God, Everlasting Father, Prince of Peace.

**Isaiah 9:6**

## RESPOND
Praise the Lord! 'Let everything that has breath praise the Lord' (Psalm 150:6).

**Bible in a year:** Nehemiah 13;  Luke 10

# Scripture Union

By purchasing *Daily Bread*, you are helping to support Scripture Union's mission with children and young people. Thank you!

Subscribe to our free supporter and prayer magazine at su.org.uk/ connectingyou

# The Time Lord

About the writer
**Gethin Russell-Jones**

Gethin is co-minister at Ararat Baptist Church, Cardiff and has served several churches over the last 32 years. Away from pastoring, he is married to Clare and they have four children and four lively grandsons. Gethin allocates the remaining hours to running slow marathons and meeting editorial deadlines.

During the platinum jubilee celebrations for the late Queen Elizabeth II in 2022, it was often repeated that 14 prime ministers had served her during her 70-year reign. This new Elizabethan age had straddled seismic political, cultural, technological and global changes. The book of Isaiah (claimed by many scholars to have been written by multiple authors) encompasses a longer period. It starts towards the end of King Uzziah's reign, who probably died around 740 BC and ends with the reign of Cyrus the Great and the Babylonian Empire (who died in about 530 BC). Spanning two centuries, it gives a bird's-eye view of God's activity in the world. By the time Isaiah begins his ministry, the northern kingdom of Israel has been captured by the Assyrian armies. Judah in the south, with its capital Jerusalem, is vulnerable to predatory neighbours.

Isaiah offers a theology of hope despite the rise of these global superpowers. In his analysis of world events, he sees the growing might of the Assyrian Empire, which in turn will be overpowered by its Babylonian rival. To the south he describes the rise of Egypt on the world stage, powered by an Ethiopian dynasty. They all see themselves as the world's leading powers, but they will be disappointed. Isaiah's imaginative genius is to see the Lord as the ruler of time and space. He is working out his purposes and one day his knowledge will fill the earth 'as the waters cover the sea' (Isaiah 11:9).

# The other Christmas reading

## PREPARE

**There are times when everything seems to be against us. Like a cruel game of dominoes, the pieces of life seem to fall down, despite our best efforts. Remember and reflect: God is for us, not against us.**

## READ

**Isaiah 9:8–21**

## EXPLORE

This uncomfortable passage is connected to one of the most popular readings of Christmas time (9:1–7). But this is the other reading, the one that is rarely heard. The earlier words of comfort have given way to judgement. The focus has shifted. The first seven verses of the chapter are addressed to people groups who feel abandoned; although they walk in darkness, a great light is about to shine upon them. But this reading speaks of judgement.

These verses are addressed to the northern kingdom of Israel, established after civil war around 930 BC. After the death of Solomon and the accession of his son, Rehoboam, the unity of the kingdom dissolved into warring factions. Ten tribes formed the new nation of Israel, leaving Judah and Benjamin as the only tribes in the south.

But why this unremitting judgement? Part of the answer appears in verse 9: their national characteristic is pride and arrogance. Instead of seeking the Lord and affirming the covenant he made with them, they have courted new political friends. If pride comes before a fall, then Israel's collapse will be deadly. How might these verses speak to our own times?

> All the people will know it – Ephraim and the inhabitants of Samaria – who say with pride and arrogance of heart...
>
> **Isaiah 9:9**

## RESPOND

Pray: Lord, I'm not as strong as I think I am. I need to know your great light breaking over me, so I humbly open my heart to you.

**Bible in a year:** Esther 1–3; Psalm 79

# I'll do it my way

## PREPARE
John Wesley was greatly influenced by a short book called *The Life of God in the Soul of Man.*** Ask God now to fill you again with his Spirit, that you may live fully the life given to you.

## READ
**Psalm 101**

## EXPLORE
Mission statements are a feature of contemporary corporate life. In a few sentences, companies articulate the reason for their existence and their business vision. They are also increasingly part of the job recruitment process. Candidates are asked to write their own mission statements, expressing their own sense of vision and purpose.

This psalm belongs to a sub-category called the 'royal psalms', where the voice belongs to the king in Jerusalem. In it he declares his own mission statement: the values and behaviours he intends to pursue as king. Verse 2 is particularly fascinating: 'I will be careful to lead a blameless life'. After asserting this intention, he pleads with God to come to him. Brueggemann and Bellinger,* in their commentary on the psalms, call this an act of insistent hope. The king is looking to God to help with delivery of his promises to be a man of integrity. It is said that the famous eighteenth-century Welsh preacher, Christmas Evans, had a similar practice. While travelling and praying on horseback, he would occasionally dismount and build a pile of rocks to show that God had come to him and given him a promise. The rocks were a sign of that agreement.

I will be careful to lead a blameless life – when will you come to me? I will conduct the affairs of my house with a blameless heart.

**Psalm 101:2**

### RESPOND
What are you asking God to help you with at present?

*W Brueggemann and W Bellinger, *Psalms: New Cambridge Bible Commentary*, Cambridge University Press, 2014
**Henry Scougal, *The Life of God in the Soul of a Man*

**Bible in a year:** Esther 4,5;  Luke 11

## Monday 17 July
### Isaiah 10:1–34

# A strange comfort

## PREPARE

In a world beset by international tension and frightening geopolitical agendas, we turn to the God of all hope and comfort. The resurrection of Jesus Christ changes everything – and one day the whole of creation will bow before him.

## READ
**Isaiah 10:1–34**

## EXPLORE

The capacity to see beyond the present moment is powerful. I once had a friend who loved fishing in a nearby estuary. He would wait for hours, knowing that eventually the tidal conditions would change, and a catch be likely. Isaiah is doing something similar here and it's a brilliant example of the way he views history.

He looks at the crisis facing Judah and its vulnerability to the advancing Assyrian forces (vs 5,6). In the same way that Israel in the north collapsed under its imperial might, so too will hapless Judah (vs 10,11). Theirs will be a hard and bitter lesson. But God's relationship with the Assyrians is complex. He sends them against his own people (v 6) but the prophet speaks woe over them (v 5). The power they wield is given to them by God and they will overreach themselves. This is a message of hope (vs 20,21). Don't be afraid of them, says the Lord; I have limited their power (v 24). Ultimately God will work it out. In the meantime we wait and hope.

> Therefore this is what the Lord, the Lord Almighty says: 'My people who live in Zion, do not be afraid of the Assyrians, who beat you with a rod and lift up a club against you, as Egypt did.'
>
> **Isaiah 10:24**

### RESPOND

'Blessed are the poor in spirit for theirs is the kingdom of heaven' (Matthew 5:3). Pray: Lord Jesus, I look to you today and lift up all who feel oppressed and overlooked. May the kingdom be theirs today. Amen.

**Bible in a year:** Esther 6,7; Luke 12

# As the waters cover the sea

## PREPARE

**Pray: Holy Spirit, open my eyes to the presence of Jesus around me: 'all things have been created through him and for him. He is before all things, and in him all things hold together' (Colossians 1:16,17).**

## READ

**Isaiah 11:1–16**

## EXPLORE

From tiny acorns, so the saying goes, mighty oaks grow. And this reading says much the same thing, albeit using a different aspect of horticulture. A shoot springing out of a stump is hardly a promising beginning, but that's what the prophet imagines.

Amid danger and calamity for Judah and Israel, something else is happening. It's small, barely noticeable, but God is bringing life out of something that seems dead. He discerns movement in a family tree, stirrings of promise in the line of King David's father, Jesse (v 1). Through his line will come one who will bring justice and fairness for the poor of the earth (v 4). I am reminded of the way justice is personified outside many law courts across the world. She carries the sword of truth in one hand and impartial scales in another. And she is often blindfolded. She dispenses her justice without fear or favour. By God's Spirit, this promised one – 'the Branch from Jesse' – will rule justly and do the right thing for the poor (vs 3,4). We have hope in him (Hebrews 6:19).

They will neither harm nor destroy on all my holy mountain, for the earth will be filled with the knowledge of the LORD as the waters cover the sea.

**Isaiah 11:9**

## RESPOND

Pray: King of the nations, Lord of the nations, the Lord who is my shepherd, I bring you my adoration and praise now.

**Bible in a year:** Esther 8–10;  Luke 13

## Wednesday 19 July
Isaiah 12:1–6

# In that day

## PREPARE
Bring to mind a song or tune that brings a sense of hope. Depending on where you are, why not hum, whistle or even sing it to the Lord, who is our salvation (v 2)?

- - - - - - - - - - - - - - - - - - - - - - - - - - - - - - - - - - - -

## READ
**Isaiah 12:1–6**

## EXPLORE
There's a song we sing regularly in our church, and it appeals to all ages. It's about God being a great big God. It says that 'he's higher than a skyscraper … deeper than a submarine' and beyond our imagination.* There are actions, and whenever the band strikes the opening chords, we're on our feet.

It works because the words are simple, and yet utterly profound. And it's got a toe-tapping tune. Isaiah surely has a song in mind here. It's a personal song, a burst of hope from a grateful heart (vs 1,2), but in the second part (vs 4–6) it transcends individuals and sweeps up the people of Israel, indeed the whole earth.

In his book *Isaiah for Everyone*,** John Goldingay sees this chapter as marking the end of the first great section in Isaiah. After a series of confrontations, warnings and judgement, the Lord is giving his people a song of hope. It's a song of the future, but it's to be sung now.

> 'Sing to the LORD, for he has done glorious things; let this be known to all the world.'
>
> **Isaiah 12:5**

## RESPOND
Imagine 'the wells of salvation' (v 3). The flowing, cool, refreshing depths of this living water. In your imagination, lay hold of a jug and fill it to the brim with this water of God's saving presence – and quench your thirst.

*Vineyard Kids, 2011
**John Goldingay, *Isaiah for Everyone*, SPCK, 2015

- - - - - - - - - - - - - - - - - - - - - - - - - - - - - - - - - - - -

**Bible in a year:** Job 1,2; Psalm 80

# Babylon's burning

## PREPARE
Pray: King of the nations, Lord of everything, I come before you now. You, whose eye is on the sparrow and who know each hair on my head. God of the small things and epic spaces, I submit to you.

## READ
**Isaiah 13:1–22**

## EXPLORE
This is the start of a new section in Isaiah's prophecy. Up until now, his prophetic utterances have mainly been spoken over Judah, Israel and Jerusalem. Now the narrative moves on and Isaiah turns his attention to the world's most powerful and dangerous rulers.

The canvas on which he paints his word pictures is on a massive scale. While he can see Judah and Israel's real-time plight, he is also able to imagine the world in the distant future. In the language of modern media devices, he fast-forwards before returning to play back. Judah will eventually fall to Babylonian rule in about a century's time (around 586 BC), but Isaiah goes beyond this and imagines that empire's own downfall (vs 19–22).

A decisive period is coming, known as the day of the Lord (vs 6,9), when Babylon will be crushed and God's people restored. On the grand stage of human history, nothing is left to fate and chance. It may look bleak for the foreseeable future, but God has not forgotten his people. He is on the move (vs 2,3). It will be painful, and generations will pass, but God has not forgotten his people.

> Wail, for the day of the LORD is near; it will come like destruction from the Almighty.
>
> **Isaiah 13:6**

## RESPOND
Pray: I lift before you, Lord, the poor and oppressed of the earth and ask that they might taste your justice and freedom.

**Bible in a year:** Job 3,4; Luke 14

## Friday 21 July
Isaiah 14:1–15

# How you have fallen

### PREPARE
'Peace, perfect peace, 'mid suffering's sharpest throes? The sympathy of Jesus breathes repose.'* Pause to be still. Breathe out the concerns you carry and, as you inhale, focus on the grace of God that is ever present.

• • • • • • • • • • • • • • • • • • • • • • • • • • • • • • • • • • • • • • • • • • • • • • • • • • •

### READ
**Isaiah 14:1–15**

### EXPLORE
Bring to mind a war that is currently happening in the world. Think of the aggression of the dominant nation and then imagine another power even greater than that one. Sounds confusing, but these are the prophetic gymnastics exercised by Isaiah. He goes beyond the present dominance of Assyria and sees the emergence of the Babylonian Empire. But there's more: they in turn will be destroyed by the Medes.

Isaiah's analysis of global power has a contemporary ring. Empires rise and fall. In the eighteenth and nineteenth centuries the British Empire asserted its rule against others, whereas we now live with the dominance of the US and China. But Isaiah has a word of warning for Babylon and maybe for all superpowers. Their fall is inevitable (v 12), or in words popularised by eighteenth-century boxer Bob Fitzsimmons, 'the bigger they are the harder they fall'. There can only be one superpower in the universe: the Lord who has mercy on his people and the poor of the earth (v 1).

> The Lord will have compassion on Jacob; once again he will choose Israel and will settle them in their own land.
>
> **Isaiah 14:1**

### RESPOND
Pray: Lord Jesus, you are our bright morning star, the 'radiance of God's glory' (Hebrews 1:3), our coming king. To you I bring my adoration as I pray for my world.

*Edward Henry Bickersteth, 1875

• • • • • • • • • • • • • • • • • • • • • • • • • • • • • • • • • • • • • • • • • • • • • • • • • • •

**Bible in a year:** Job 5,6;  Luke 15

# Love your 'frenemies'

## PREPARE
In a 24-hour news agenda dominated by vying powers, turn to another throne. Let's gaze at the seat of all power and authority, in heaven and on earth, on which sits the king of love, justice and fairness.

· · · · · · · · · · · · · · · · · · · · · · · · · · · · · · · · · · · · · · · · · · · · · · · · · · · · · · · · · · · · · · · · · · · · · · · ·

## READ
**Isaiah 15:1 – 16:14**

## EXPLORE
Isaiah's attention now turns to a much closer neighbour, Moab. Lying east along the Jordan, Judah and the northern kingdom of Israel had a complicated relationship with Moab. Under King David, Israel ruled over this territory, but the civil war saw them isolated against other enemies. The origin of its story is given in Genesis 19, where the child born out of incest between Lot and his daughter is named Moab.

During the nation's desert wanderings, Balak, king of Moab, hires Balaam to curse them (Numbers 22). But the Moabites are also presented in a more favourable light. For example, the book of Ruth tells the story of the young Moabite woman whose character and faith in the God of Israel and her lifestyle are celebrated (eg Ruth 3:11,12). In modern parlance, Moab was a 'frenemy' (friend and enemy). The prophet calls the Moabites back into friendship with Judah by telling them to send tribute to Jerusalem (16:1), to enjoy the protection and rule that will once again flow from the throne of David (16:5).

In love a throne will be established; in faithfulness a man will sit on it … one who in judging seeks justice and speeds the cause of righteousness.

**Isaiah 16:5**

## RESPOND
Pray for those you find difficult to love, with whom you have a complex relationship. This may be hard to do, but pray that God will bless them.

· · · · · · · · · · · · · · · · · · · · · · · · · · · · · · · · · · · · · · · · · · · · · · · · · · · · · · · · · · · · · · · · · · · · · · · ·

**Bible in a year:** Job 7,8;  Psalms 81,82

# Listen to me, Lord

## PREPARE

**Where do you need God's help now? Maybe you need him to bring reassurance or intervene in some way, or maybe you want him to move in someone else's life. Let him hear your cry for help.**

## READ

**Psalm 102**

## EXPLORE

This psalm is the fifth of the so-called penitential psalms (Psalms 6; 32; 38; 51; 102; 130; 143). They have been given this title because of their use in church liturgy at the beginning of the season of Lent on Ash Wednesday. Its superscription (the words which introduce the psalm in verse 1) identifies the writer's state of mind. He feels afflicted and weak; this is his lament.

Some commentators see this psalm as the words of the king, while others date it to a time when the nation is in exile and the psalmist is lamenting his nation's losses. But our attention is drawn to the poet's spiritual and emotional condition. He is not in a good way, and he pours out a lament. Lament is not a popular genre within modern worship. We generally like our songs to be happy, even triumphant.

But there are many psalms of lament in the collection we have – almost a third. These are sometimes of a personal nature (eg Psalm 86) and at other times express the grievances of a community (eg Psalm 12). Just as loss is inevitable in our lives, so must lament form a regular part of our personal and corporate worship.

Hear my prayer, LORD; let my cry for help come to you.

**Psalm 102:1**

---

## RESPOND

Take time to pour out your deepest cries and laments to the Lord.

---

**Bible in a year:** Job 9,10; Luke 16

# The long wait

## PREPARE

**There are times when we sense God's presence keenly; there are periods when he seems absent, even though he is not. Pause to be still, and in the stillness wait for the Lord's still, small voice.**

## READ

**Isaiah 17:1 – 18:7**

## EXPLORE

These two chapters offer another bird's-eye prophetic tour, this time of lesser superpowers in the ancient world (Damascus, Cush). It seems unlikely that Isaiah was widely travelled, but his work in Jerusalem seems to have given him an extensive knowledge of current affairs.

Chapter 18 provides an eye-witness account of a doomed strategic alliance. Judah's southern neighbour, Egypt, is ruled by a powerful Ethiopian elite. It's amassing support for a strike on the Assyrians and elicits the support of their Judean neighbours. And Isaiah appears to have witnessed their envoys' arrival in Jerusalem. He speaks of a 'people tall and smooth-skinned', their papyrus ships, a land of many rivers and a strange language (18:2).

Some commentators wonder if Isaiah had seen their arrival in the southern port of Eilat in the Gulf of Aqaba. It reads like a first-hand account. This alliance never happens, but God's reaction, as described by Isaiah, is intriguing. He plays a waiting game (18:4), silently watching in the shimmering heat to see what transpires. There are times when his power is revealed in silence, which may even *feel* like his absence.

... 'I will remain quiet and will look on from my dwelling place, like shimmering heat in the sunshine, like a cloud of dew in the heat of harvest.'

**Isaiah 18:4**

## RESPOND

Pray: In my waiting, I wait on you.
In my wrestling, I wrestle with you.
In my silence, I trust in you.

**Bible in a year:** Job 11,12; Luke 17

## Tuesday 25 July

Isaiah 19:1–25

# God's strange ways

## PREPARE

'As the heavens are higher than the earth, so are my ways higher than your ways and my thoughts than your thoughts' (Isaiah 55:9). Pause and meditate on God's loving, mysterious and sometimes hidden care.

## READ

**Isaiah 19:1–25**

## EXPLORE

The late Rabbi Lord Jonathan Sacks spent his life promoting dialogue between the great Abrahamic faiths, Judaism, Islam and Christianity. In his book *Not in God's Name*,* he writes of these often difficult relationships in terms of a family feud. Drawing on some of the great family stories of the Old Testament, he argues that God's reconciling ways can be seen in the most bitter family disputes.

This reading ends on an even more controversial note. After multiple chapters of judgement against Assyria and Egypt, God offers a surprising resolution. After a period of judgement, Egypt will turn back to the Lord, and Assyria will join them in common worship. A highway of praise will connect these warring nations and God's blessing will not be restricted to Israel but shared with Egypt and Assyria (vs 23–25).

This vision of universal peace and fellowship has already been seen in Isaiah (2:4), but this closing verse has a tender ring to it. After judgement comes healing and the Gentiles (us?) will be fully included in God's kingdom.

... 'Blessed be Egypt my people, Assyria my handiwork, and Israel my inheritance.'

**Isaiah 19:25**

---

## RESPOND

'He came and preached peace to you who were far away and peace to those who were near. For through him we both have access to the Father by one Spirit' (Ephesians 2:17,18). Give thanks for God's reconciling love.

---

*Jonathan Sacks, *Not in God's Name*, Hodder & Stoughton, 2015

**Bible in a year:** Job 13,14; Luke 18

# Body score

## PREPARE
Pause... Become aware of your environment and your breathing. Take note of how you are feeling today. Pray: Lord, I offer myself to you.

..................................................................................

## READ
Isaiah 20:1 – 21:17

## EXPLORE
In his book *Body Keeps the Score*, Bessel van der Kolk writes about the impact of trauma on the body. Traumatic events often leave a trail of physical and mental pain in our lives, and he speaks movingly of his therapeutic work among those afflicted. Isaiah, in chapter 20, is asked by the Lord to use his body prophetically. Not by way of speech, or even actions, but in the removal of certain clothing (20:2).

Taking away his sackcloth may have been a sign of vulnerability. John Goldingay suggests that sackcloth was normally worn at home, a kind of comfort wear not appropriate in public spaces. As a sign of poverty, Isaiah was making a point about the spiritual state of the nation. In its removal, this becomes a sign of Israel's weakness against Assyrian might. For three years, Isaiah wears only his underwear and walks barefoot among the people.

God's judgement is coming on Egypt and Ethiopia; Israel will be exposed to the great superpower of Assyria. Isaiah's body tells the story of his nation's parlous state.

In chapter 21, Isaiah reflects on the bigger context of the international situation. There are warnings here for God's people, yet also assurances of God's knowledge and vigilance.

'See what has happened to those we relied on ... How then can we escape?'

**Isaiah 20:6**

---

### RESPOND
Give thanks for the ministry of reconciliation: in Christ 'God was reconciling the world to himself ... not counting people's sins against them' (2 Corinthians 5:19).

---

..................................................................................

**Bible in a year:** Job 15–17;  Psalms 83,84

# "I DON'T GO TO CHURCH BUT..."

**95%** of under-18s don't go to church. **BUT** many are open to faith.

Together we can reach them!

SCAN TO JOIN **THE 95** CAMPAIGN FOR FREE

# Jesus sat down

While I was writing these notes, a friend told me about his love of the book of Hebrews. So much so that he was studying it with a friend who is exploring Christianity. From a Jewish background, she is interested in the writer's reliance upon the Old Testament.

People usually use the Gospels to introduce people to Jesus. Hebrews, however, complements their picture of Jesus. For example, Jesus sat down to teach, as was the custom: in the Temple (Luke 2), in a local synagogue (Luke 4), in a boat (Luke 5), on a hillside (Matthew 5), by a well (John 4) and in a home (John 11). Hebrews focuses on different reasons for being seated: on a throne and at the Father's right hand (Hebrews 10:12; 12:2). Jesus sits to reign as King. He also sits as a priest because his one sacrifice makes all others irrelevant. The 'seated Jesus' has shaped these notes.

Theories of the writer's identity abound, including that she was a woman. Whoever they were, they knew the Old Testament Scriptures. With a pastoral heart, they longed that the readers, who had known persecution (10:32–35), would refuse to be distracted from deepening their relationship with Jesus.

I have found myself drawn into the presence of the ascended Christ as I've been immersed in Hebrews. I hope you'll join with me in being captivated by the vision of Jesus that this writer offers.

PS: Try to read all eight chapters in one sitting and, at the end of this series, read the last five!

**About the writer**
**Ro Willoughby**

For many years, Ro was an editor with Scripture Union. She is now a lay minister at St Chad's Woodseats, Sheffield, engaging with people of all ages. During 2022 in Oberammergau, Germany, along with half a million others, she was captivated by the powerful retelling of the last week of Jesus' life.

# Seated on the throne

## PREPARE
**Think about Jesus' ascension into heaven. What picture comes to mind? A pair of feet disappearing into a cloud?! Ask God to refresh your understanding of the ascension.**

## READ
**Hebrews 1:1–4**

## EXPLORE
Five days ago, it was the Feast of the Ascension. That day I met with a group of Christians who didn't realise what day it was. They wondered why I wanted to celebrate Jesus' ascension that evening.

The writer of Hebrews would want to enlighten them. These opening verses offer a brief account of Jesus' life leading to his return to heaven. He existed long before the world began, but now is described as the perfect, final imprint of God's very being (v 3). His death and resurrection completed his mission on earth. His resurrection body with its limitations was no longer needed. Job done! Time for the Spirit to come instead.

Jesus' ascension means that as an equal and greater than the angels, he can sit down beside his Father. Far from putting his feet up, he's doing many things including sustaining all things by his word. And he doesn't remain seated. Moments before his death (Acts 7:56), Stephen saw Jesus standing at the right hand of his Father, ready to welcome him.

> After he had provided purification for sins, he sat down at the right hand of the Majesty in heaven.
>
> **Hebrews 1:3**

## RESPOND
Reflect on Jesus' death, resurrection, ascension and reign in heaven now the Spirit has come. Which of these events matters most to you, or are they intertwined? Talk with God about what it means to you that Jesus' work on earth is complete.

**Bible in a year:** Job 18,19;  Luke 19

# Identified as God's Son

## PREPARE
**Ideas of monarchy and political systems are shaped by fairy tales, stories from history and contemporary experiences of royalty. When we sing of 'Jesus as King', what do you think about?**

## READ
**Hebrews 1:5–14**

## EXPLORE
In June 2022 the UK celebrated the late Queen Elizabeth's platinum jubilee. Increasingly, as she became more frail, she passed duties on to her son, Charles. But her authority as monarch remained.

This is different from the authority the Father grants to his Son. The right hand is the place of honour (vs 3,13). The writer uses references, mainly from the psalms, to expand on this authority. For example, through the words of Psalm 2:7 (see v 5), he sees Jesus, sitting at the Father's side in heaven (v 3) – his identity as the Son of God revealed (see yesterday's note). On earth Jesus had submitted to the authority of the Father, willingly emptying himself (Philippians 2:7). But always, eternally, he is God's Son (eg Matthew 3:17).

Notice what God says about Jesus' throne and everything that it stands for (vs 8,9; see Psalm 45:6,7). All this is accompanied by celebratory anointing and activity. God pours even more accolades upon his Son's head (vs 10–13). Take time to reflect upon each of these. No human coronation comes anywhere near to this. God the Father and God the Son reign together.

To which of the angels did God ever say, 'Sit at my right hand until I make your enemies a footstool for your feet'?

**Hebrews 1:13**

## RESPOND
The old chorus 'Yesterday, today, for ever' includes the words, 'All may change, but Jesus never' (AB Simpson, 1843–1919). Tell God what today's unimaginable descriptions of Jesus mean to you.

**Bible in a year:** Job 20,21;  Luke 20

# Made lower than the angels

## PREPARE
Look back to Thursday's reading and ask Jesus to make you curious, to stretch your understanding of him a bit more (v 9).

. . . . . . . . . . . . . . . . . . . . . . . . . . . . . . . . . . . . . . . . . . . . . . . . . . .

## READ
**Hebrews 2:1–9**

## EXPLORE
I've always liked Psalm 8, because of the dignity God has given to human beings, just 'a little lower than the angels … [to be] rulers over the works of your [God's] hands' (Psalm 8:5,6). We, like the readers of Hebrews, might wonder why the writer quotes from Psalm 8. In effect, the timeline pattern of 1:1–4 is being repeated.

God commanded Adam and Eve to be stewards of his world (Psalm 8:6–8; Genesis 1:26–28). They failed. The place of humans in creation is one of fallen failure, as the climate crisis and global conflicts constantly remind us. We do not yet see human beings as they were meant to be (v 8). But we will. A glorious hope.

That does not prevent us seeing Jesus. In becoming human, he became lower than the angels. It was this that enabled him to taste death for everyone. Jesus has now gone higher, crowned with glory and honour, seated at God's right hand, waiting for the end of time when his enemies will be placed beneath his feet (1:13; see Psalm 110:1).

> But we do see Jesus, who was made lower than the angels for a little while, now crowned with glory and honour…
>
> **Hebrews 2:9**

## RESPOND
We focus upon Christ, not angels. Pause to 'see' Jesus in all his glory – having tasted death, now crowned, seated beside his Father, reigning and sustaining his world. Maybe you'll need to breathe in deeply as you tentatively grasp the impossible.

. . . . . . . . . . . . . . . . . . . . . . . . . . . . . . . . . . . . . . . . . . . . . . . . . . .

**Bible in a year:** Job 22,23;  Psalm 85

# God made known

## PREPARE

If someone asked you which is the one characteristic of God you most appreciate, what would you say?

........................................................................................

## READ

**Psalm 103**

## EXPLORE

Becoming immersed in Hebrews has sometimes so overwhelmed me that I've had to take a break. There's too much of Christ to take in. Psalm 103 continues in the same vein, though for the writer Christ himself has not yet become lower than the angels!

The book of Hebrews begins by declaring that God has spoken in many ways in the past. This psalm reminds us of what God has done for his people long before Christ. Which of these actions of God strike you in particular? We're also reminded that God communicated directly with Moses (v 7) – throughout the people's wanderings in the wilderness, but especially when he was given the Law on Mount Sinai. Yet it's not just about God's deeds. It is his character that is central – abounding, never-ending love, compassion and knowledge (eg vs 13,17).

Just knowing facts about God and his deeds was never sufficient for anyone to begin to 'know' God. So finally, he spoke by his Son (Hebrews 1:2). Read through this psalm again. In what ways does Jesus make God known by his words and actions during his earthly life? What about now, seated at the right hand of the Father (Hebrews 1:3)?

The LORD has established his throne in heaven, and his kingdom rules over all.

**Psalm 103:19**

## RESPOND

'No one has ever seen God, but the one and only Son, who is himself God and is in the closest relationship with the Father, has made him known' (John 1:18). Thank God for Jesus!

........................................................................................

**Bible in a year:** Job 24–26;  Luke 21

## Monday 31 July
### Hebrews 2:10–18

# Victorious pioneer

## PREPARE
**Do you think of Jesus as your Lord, master, friend, Saviour, brother, role model or...?**

## READ
**Hebrews 2:10–18**

## EXPLORE
As I write, it is the season for final football league and cup matches in the UK. These culminate in the victorious captain (not the manager) receiving the trophy and leading the team in their celebratory triumph. The captain has been through it all with the players.

Jesus has suffered for the sake of all those whom he comes to call his brothers and sisters (v 12). His suffering has enabled them to be made holy as he is holy (vs 10,11). By virtue of being a sibling of Christ they have become a son or daughter of God. (This is different language from Paul's use of the concept of adoption: see, for example, Ephesians 1:5; Romans 8:15.)

Jesus' ultimate goal as the ascended and exalted Christ was to be the pioneer of salvation, leading his brothers and sisters into God's eternal presence (v 10). He played and won the match single-handedly. He has earned the right to lead his 'team' in their victory march.

The writer expands on the consequences of Jesus' human suffering. The one who holds the power of death is utterly crushed. Death's terrifying stranglehold is destroyed (vs 14,15). Jesus has been through it all. Remember his terror in Gethsemane and on the cross (Luke 22:42,44; Mark 15:34)!

> Jesus is not ashamed to call them brothers and sisters.
>
> **Hebrews 2:11**

## RESPOND
If you or someone you know are going through a tough time, remember that Jesus has been there before us. Pray in the light of that.

**Bible in a year:** Job 27,28; Luke 22

# Greater than Moses

## PREPARE
We share friendships and a common purpose with groups of people. But life is busy. We get distracted. Over time, relationships fragment; their significance diminishes. How easily can that happen to our relationship with Christ?

....................................................................

## READ
**Hebrews 3:1–19**

## EXPLORE
Until Christ came, no one had ever surpassed Moses as the person through whom God communicated with his people. The writer makes a comparison between Moses and Jesus by saying that God's people were 'God's house'. God called Moses 'faithful in all my house', rebuking Aaron and Miriam for not taking their brother Moses seriously (Numbers 12:7). Moses may have been the steward of this house, but Christ is far more. He is its creator and builder.

Moses had to contend with the rebellious behaviour of God's people in the wilderness, belligerently testing God, as the quotation from Psalm 95 describes (vs 8–11). This leads the writer to urge readers who have accepted the salvation of Christ to persevere, so that there is 'no evil unbelief lying around that will trip you up and throw you off course, diverting you from the living God' (vs 12–14, *The Message*). Like the people of Israel, they too could come under God's judgement.

These are serious words. The ascended Jesus calls for our full attention (v 1) for we are not only at home in the 'house' Jesus built, but we have become his younger brothers and sisters (2:11; 3:1).

Holy brothers and sisters, who share in the heavenly calling, fix your thoughts on Jesus...

**Hebrews 3:1**

## RESPOND
Use verses 6 and 14 to help you begin a conversation with God.

....................................................................

**Bible in a year:** Job 29,30; Luke 23

# Wednesday 2 August
Hebrews 4:1–13

# Promises a place of rest

## PREPARE
Psalm 95 features again in today's verses, so read the whole psalm in its entirety as you prepare to hear God (v 7): 'Today, if only you would hear his voice' (Psalm 95:7).

## READ
**Hebrews 4:1–13**

## EXPLORE
The letter to the Hebrews begins with God speaking to the prophets, through Moses, the psalms, David and ultimately through the Son. Verses 12 and 13 in today's passage conclude the first section of this letter. The penetration of his Word is awesomely powerful (vs 12,13).

But has the writer's needle got stuck? How many times is Psalm 95 quoted? God rested, having finished his work of creation (v 3). Job done! Similarly, Jesus, also involved in creation, ascended into heaven, sat down on his throne (1:3). Job done!

But God the Father, Son and Spirit is certainly not inactive. This 'rest' is not a 'state of being' but a 'real place' of activity and celebration. Here is the urgent invitation to God's people to persevere, to be found worthy to enter the place that the writer describes in promised land language (v 11). For example, 'rest' in these verses is similar to the idea of 'city' or 'homeland' in 11:9,10,13–16; 12:22. This is the promised destiny of anyone who obeys and trusts God (vs 1,2).

> Now we who have believed enter that rest...

**Hebrews 4:3**

## RESPOND
This is your destiny. 'Our citizenship is in heaven. And we eagerly await a Saviour from there ... who ... will transform our lowly bodies so that they will be like his glorious body' (Philippians 3:20,21). Reflect on this, our hope!

**Bible in a year:** Job 31,32; Psalms 86,87

# Fully human like us

## PREPARE
Actions have consequences. Usually we don't know what significance our actions might have. Identify something you've said or done recently that has had consequences (good or bad).

. . . . . . . . . . . . . . . . . . . . . . . . . . . . . . . . . . . . . . . . . . . . . . . . . . . .

## READ
**Hebrews 4:14 – 5:10**

## EXPLORE
The writer identifies two actions with profoundly eternal consequences. First, our great high priest has gone through the heavens and, as we know, has sat down at the Father's side (v 14). That means that we (which includes this writer) can be 100 per cent confident that all we know about Jesus is true. He really has made us acceptable to God.

Secondly, this high priest, called by God (as all priests), has experienced the weakness and limitations of being fully human (v 15). However, Jesus has remained fully obedient to God, unlike every other priest, including Aaron (v 4) who played a prominent part in leading the Israelites astray in the wilderness (Exodus 32). The consequence of this is that, although we know we are sinners, we don't need to fear we're not good enough for God. God the Son understands the temptations that beset our humanity. He remains our eternal role model. Yet, there is no need to tiptoe timidly into God's presence. His merciful grace is available to every one of us in our fallen state (v 16).

Therefore, since we have a great high priest who has ascended into heaven, Jesus the Son of God, let us hold firmly to the faith we profess.

**Hebrews 4:14**

### RESPOND
Which of your human weaknesses particularly troubles you? How hard is it to accept that Jesus sympathises with you and that God's merciful forgiveness is simply waiting to be received? Boldly open up a conversation with God.

. . . . . . . . . . . . . . . . . . . . . . . . . . . . . . . . . . . . . . . . . . . . . . . . . . . .

**Bible in a year:** Job 33,34;  Luke 24

# Friday 4 August

Hebrews 5:11 – 6:12

# What we know about Jesus

## PREPARE

Time for a spiritual health check! How much has your desire to know God deepened this past year? Ask him to unblock your ears to hear his voice.

. . . . . . . . . . . . . . . . . . . . . . . . . . . . . . . . . . . . . . . . . . . . . . . . . . .

## READ

**Hebrews 5:11 – 6:12**

## EXPLORE

After a day at school, young children are physically and mentally too tired to learn anything more, though their curiosity is not dulled. The hardness of heart of God's people in Psalm 95 was unlike this, for theirs was a deliberate refusal to listen or learn.

The dullness referred to in 5:11 is different again. The writer reassures readers that God remembers how they've shown their love for him (6:10), but also tells them that they're not making any effort to understand more. They need to move beyond the basics to a deeper, mature faith (6:1). They've got teeth, so they need to learn to chew on solid spiritual food (5:14). This letter is packed with a rich, nourishing diet of truths about Jesus.

This comes with a warning of danger. It is still possible for someone who has tasted the wonder of belonging to God to then refuse to learn from the teachings about Christ (6:4–6). There is no way back for anyone remaining in a state of persistent, deliberate disobedience – no hope of repentance (10:26). This passage is describing hardened and fierce opponents of Christ, not sensitive believers struggling with occasional or even frequent spiritual failure (see Matthew 12:31,32).

But solid food is for the mature, who by constant use have trained themselves to distinguish good from evil.

**Hebrews 5:14**

## RESPOND

How rich and varied is your spiritual diet? How determined are you to dig deeper, so that your faith continues to mature? God makes himself known to those who seek him.

. . . . . . . . . . . . . . . . . . . . . . . . . . . . . . . . . . . . . . . . . . . . . . . . . . .

**Bible in a year:** Job 35,36; Philippians 1

# Provides a place of safety

## PREPARE
It is too easy for politicians to make promises for the future that they cannot fulfil. That can make us cynical or insecure. Who can we trust?

## READ
**Hebrews 6:13–20**

## EXPLORE
I am writing in the early summer when conditions in the English Channel encourage refugees to risk crossing the busiest shipping channel in the world in overloaded, flimsy boats. They are so desperate to enter the UK, longing for something better. They have no guarantee of gaining it.

This contrasts with the image in Hebrews of Christian hope which is 100 per cent secure. When God makes an oath, it is inevitably guaranteed. There is nothing and 'no one greater' than he to deflect or water down his promises (v 13). The writer illustrates this truth with reference to God's guaranteed promises made to Abraham. Abraham's grounds for confident hope will reappear in 11:8–19.

The writer builds on his insistence that God's people need to persevere as they journey with God – who have 'fled to take hold of the hope set before us' (v 18) – so that they too can be certain of entering God's presence. A firm, reliable anchor prevents a drifting away (v 19). Very beautifully, we're told that Jesus has already arrived to welcome us to this place of safety (v 20).

## We have this hope as an anchor for the soul, firm and secure.
**Hebrews 6:19**

## RESPOND
It is appropriate to pray for God to protect those fleeing from danger hoping to find a place of safety. Ask God to make himself known to them. Find time to reflect on what it means to you that God's promises are 100 per cent safe.

## Sunday 6 August
### Psalm 104

# Praise the Lord, O my soul!

## PREPARE
How often do you look out on God's world to sigh with sorrow, confusion or despair? Ask God to remind you that, despite everything, this is still his world. He has not left us rudderless.

· · · · · · · · · · · · · · · · · · · · · · · · · · · · · · · · · · · · · · · · · · · · · · · · · · · · · · · · · · · · · · · ·

## READ
**Psalm 104**

## EXPLORE
I knew I needed to spend time talking with God. There was so much evil going on in our world which left me bewildered and distressed. I didn't know where to start. So, I went out for a long walk, putting in my earphones to listen to songs from a worship album. My head was filled with truths about God. Before long, oblivious of passers-by, I was singing out loud, declaring the wonders of God!

Speaking out or singing this psalm would have had the same effect. Pause to picture each of the images of God's work in creation that we find in verses 1 to 9. But he has not set the world in motion to then leave it alone. Verses 10 to 32 make it clear that he is present everywhere, all the time, continuing to keep the world running.

Then, in verses 33 to 35, we return to the psalmist who reminds us to continue recalling and rejoicing over everything God has done, is doing and will do. He is fully aware of the appalling wickedness in his world (v 35). In his eternal time, it will be swept from the earth. Rehearsing all these truths comforts me and gives me hope.

I will sing to the LORD all my life; I will sing praise to my God as long as I live.

**Psalm 104:33**

## RESPOND
Praise the Lord with all that is within you!

· · · · · · · · · · · · · · · · · · · · · · · · · · · · · · · · · · · · · · · · · · · · · · · · · · · · · · · · · · · · · · · ·

**Bible in a year:** Job 39,40; Philippians 2

# Top of the pecking order

## PREPARE
The phrase 'pecking order' describes hierarchy among poultry, but it is also used to describe human hierarchies! What experience do you have of hierarchies? Reflect on what you think about them.

. . . . . . . . . . . . . . . . . . . . . . . . . . . . . . . . . . . . . . . . . . . . . . . . . . . . .

## READ
Hebrews 7:1–10

## EXPLORE
Recently I saw the Passion Play at Oberammergau in Germany, which powerfully portrays the last week of Jesus' life. The storyline is interrupted by choral music and a series of Old Testament tableaux of frozen actors. These make parallels between events in the Old Testament and those in Jesus' passion. The writer does something like this here.

Melchizedek's existence has been heralded earlier in Hebrews (5:6). You can read about his encounter with Abraham in Genesis 14:18–20. The writer introduces this mysterious figure, a king of righteousness and of peace, suggestive of the Messiah (v 2). He has no beginning or end, which suggests divinity (v 3). He appears long before the Levitical priesthood was established through Aaron, whose ancestor Levi was one of Abraham's great grandsons (v 10). Thus, Melchizedek's priesthood precedes the Levitical one which makes it superior. Abraham acknowledges this superiority by the tithing of his gifts (vs 4–6).

Sent by God, Melchizedek bestows God's blessing upon Abraham (v 1). The writer uses this encounter with Abraham to shed light on Jesus' priesthood. He presents Melchizedek as one who foreshadows Jesus (6:20). Even though Jesus existed before the beginning of time, he was not without a father or mother. He is greater than Melchizedek (v 17).

## This Melchizedek was king of Salem and priest of God Most High.
**Hebrews 7:1**

## RESPOND
What does it mean to you that Jesus is greater than any other? How does that affect the way you live?

. . . . . . . . . . . . . . . . . . . . . . . . . . . . . . . . . . . . . . . . . . . . . . . . . . . . .

**Bible in a year:** Job 41,42; Philippians 3

## Tuesday 8 August
### Hebrews 7:11–28

# The perfect priest

**PREPARE**
In Hebrews 4:15 we read that Jesus was tempted in every way, but he did not sin. What do you understand by that?

......................................................................................

**READ**
**Hebrews 7:11–28**

**EXPLORE**
In the Passion Play at Oberammergau, Caiaphas, the high priest, along with other priests, treats the claims Jesus makes for himself with disgusted incomprehension. Nicodemus and Joseph of Arimathea stand up for Jesus. This priestly class reflects the inherent weakness of the Levitical priesthood (vs 11,28): 'men in all their weakness'.

Jesus as the great high priest surpassed the old priesthood. The writer describes their differences. Descendants from the tribe of Levi inherited the right to be a priest in Israel. Yet Jesus came from the tribe of Judah. Both Jesus and Melchizedek pre-existed Levi (7:10). Jesus' qualifications for priesthood had nothing to do with inheritance enforced by the flawed law (vs 14,16). His perfect priesthood was a result of 'the power of an indestructible life (vs 16,21). It never needed to be replaced. God had sworn an oath establishing and guaranteeing it. This was foretold in Psalm 110:4, which forms the basis of the writer's argument.

A priest performing a sacrifice never sat down. No sacrifice was sufficient (10:11). Jesus' death achieved what the old system could never do. Jesus could sit down (1:3). Everything has changed. Everything is gloriously new. We can now come into God's presence (v 25).

## 'The Lord has sworn and will not change his mind: "You are a priest for ever."'
**Hebrews 7:21**

**RESPOND**
Read verses 25 to 28 again and choose one aspect of what Jesus achieved and now does. Thank God for that.

......................................................................................

**Bible in a year:** Proverbs 1,2; Philippians 4

# Makes everything new

## PREPARE
Look back over your reflections in these eight chapters. Have you been captivated by the ascended Jesus? What has made the most impact?

······································································

## READ
**Hebrews 8:1–13**

## EXPLORE
We attend a dress rehearsal, but the real thing is yet to come. Refugees living in a camp hope for something better than their temporary home. A couple engaged to be married know the best is yet to come. Until Christ's death, God's people unknowingly had to settle for the second best. Jesus has made it possible to enjoy a taste of the best NOW. But the very best in eternity is yet to come.

Verses 8 to 12 are a direct quote from Jeremiah 31:31–34 and go back to the time when Jeremiah's home city, Jerusalem, was about to be razed to the ground and its inhabitants taken as captives to Babylon. They had disobeyed God. His words, through Jeremiah, offered future hope of transformed lives, an assurance of truly knowing God (Jeremiah 31:31–34). Their sins would be forgiven, in a way they'd never experienced before. (See also 10:16,17.)

That time has now come. Jesus, seated as a priest to the right of his Father (v 1), serves to make purification for sins (1:3), interceding for us (7:25) and offering forgiveness written in a new way, in minds and hearts. We, like the readers, can experience this NOW. But the very best is yet to come (v 13).

'The days are coming ... when I will make a new covenant with the people of Israel and with the people of Judah.'
**Hebrews 8:8**

## RESPOND
The writer has been constantly urging readers to persevere and embrace a confident hope, expecting the best. Tell God what you think about this. Be thankful!

······································································

**Bible in a year:** Proverbs 3,4;  Psalm 89

# WAY IN
## Hebrews 9–13

# In Christ alone...

About the writer
**Gill Robertson**

Gill is a 60-something, recently retired vicar's wife, stepmother and fairly new grandmother; and a Lay Reader (LLM). She is also a musician, composer, crafter and cook; and the time spent on these activities is inversely proportional to that spent on housework!

*Tom Wright, *Hebrews for Everyone*, SPCK, 2003

As I write these notes, we are living in a building site. The house we moved to in early 2021 is having some alterations done to make our kitchen and dining room much more user-friendly, and to give us more storage. This involves a great deal of mess (thick, black dust everywhere), noise and upheaval. It also involves moving stuff out of two bedrooms upstairs so the electricians can put the new downstairs lighting in. Fortunately, our builders are exceedingly friendly, obliging and considerate people!

I'm in good company using this analogy. Tom Wright, in *Hebrews for Everyone*,* writes of something similar (a construction project to improve traffic flow) as he explores Hebrews chapter 9. He says, 'God has all along had a master plan for how the world would be put to rights'. The old covenant was not meant to be the finished article. The chapters ahead of us for the next couple of weeks or so look into how that inadequate, temporary model was fulfilled by the completely adequate new covenant, and how that informs and affects who we are as believers and disciples.

Hebrews has something of a reputation for being theologically dense. To be fair, some of it *is* complicated, and notes like these don't allow for greater depth, or comment, on absolutely everything. But I do pray that they will offer a fresh perspective – a new doorway, if you like – into understanding something more of Hebrews. Just like we've got into our new kitchen-diner!

# That was then...

## PREPARE

'In Christ alone my hope is found, he is my light, my strength, my song...'* Worship the Lord for all he means to you.

## READ

**Hebrews 9:1–10**

## EXPLORE

The tone in which these verses are written reminds me (somewhat) of a salesperson explaining to a customer about the previous model of their product – before launching into their sales pitch for the vastly superior new model (tomorrow!). The author of Hebrews (about whom scholars speculate but arrive at no definite conclusions) has a thorough knowledge of the old covenant tabernacle: its construction, its contents and its repetitive sacrifices. Its portable design came from the Lord himself, so that in their wanderings the Israelites would have the presence of God with them at all times (see Exodus 25:8).

However, the writer is very clear about the ultimate inadequacy of all that. Jeremiah prophesies about what was to come – a new covenant of mind and heart, with God known by all (Jeremiah 31:33,34). The tabernacle was never intended to be permanent; it was a picture, or a shadow, of what was to come, and only sufficed until then. And perhaps most importantly, it could never accomplish the deeper work that the sacrifice of Christ enables (v 9).

## ... the way into the Most Holy Place had not yet been disclosed...

**Hebrews 9:8**

## RESPOND

For some people, faith can be very much God-focused – which is of course not a bad thing! But salvation and forgiveness are found in and through Jesus. Pray for anyone you know whose faith needs to move on to a relationship with him.

*Stuart Townend and Keith Getty, copyright © 2001, Thankyou Music

**Bible in a year:** Proverbs 5,6;  Colossians 1

# Friday 11 August
## Hebrews 9:11–28

# This is now!

## PREPARE
The drawing of the unbridgeable gap, with 'Me' on one side and 'God' on the other, explains how sin separates us; then the cross is drawn in to show who brings us back together. What other images come to mind?

. . . . . . . . . . . . . . . . . . . . . . . . . . . . . . . . . . . . . . . . . . . . .

## READ
**Hebrews 9:11–28**

## EXPLORE
Now, our salesperson/author moves on to the new, improved product! The passage focuses on the power of the blood of Christ (v 14). The sacrifices made year after year by the high priest, who offered animal blood in an earthly sanctuary, only achieved outward, temporary cleansing (v 13). Compared with that, Jesus enters the heavenly sanctuary with his own blood – and it's a once and for ever deal (v 28). Jesus' sacrifice of himself achieves permanent and ongoing cleansing from sin, which reaches into the depths of who we are to bring life and forgiveness and restoration (vs 14,15). How wonderful to know.

And the purpose (v 14)? It's not a deal which, once it's done, can just be left behind and forgotten. It has implications and consequences; our salvation is *for* something: 'that we may serve…'.

It encourages us into a life where the knowledge that we belong to God, not to ourselves, makes all the difference to our identity. It projects us into a life given over to God in gratitude and service, in whatever way he chooses for us.

> How much more, then, will the blood of Christ … cleanse our consciences from acts that lead to death, so that we may serve the living God!
>
> **Hebrews 9:14**

## RESPOND
Think about the ways you are serving God at the moment. Offer them again to the Lord and ask him for his continuing guidance as you live out your salvation.

. . . . . . . . . . . . . . . . . . . . . . . . . . . . . . . . . . . . . . . . . . . . .

**Bible in a year:** Proverbs 7,8;  Colossians 2

# Perfect and holy

## PREPARE
Call to mind a time when you had to decide whether to do something really difficult or costly. How did you approach the decision? What did you do?

## READ
**Hebrews 10:1–10**

## EXPLORE
This passage continues to compare the different natures of the sacrifices of the old covenant with that of Jesus. The author writes, with reference to Psalm 40, that God was not pleased with all the animal sacrifices (v 4) – the implication being that he was pleased with the sacrifice of himself that Jesus made. Another difference is that the animals involved had no choice. Jesus, however, made a personal choice to sacrifice himself on our behalf. The cost of choosing to do that is clearly seen in the accounts of Gethsemane, when he pleaded, 'Take this cup from me.' Still he submitted himself to his Father's will and purpose (Mark 14:36).

I find verse 2 really interesting. It says that for all who have found salvation in Christ (ie 'cleansed once for all'), there is no longer any need to feel guilty for our sins. That's the difference between Christ's sacrifice and Old Testament sacrifice. Once dealt with, our transgressions are removed far from us (Psalm 103:12).

> ... we have been made holy through the sacrifice of the body of Jesus Christ once for all.
>
> **Hebrews 10:10**

## RESPOND
Pray today for anyone who is haunted by the memory of past sin and finds it hard to receive the forgiveness that is theirs. Pray they find that, while memories may remain, complete freedom from guilt is ours in Christ.

**Bible in a year:** Proverbs 9,10; Psalm 90

# Sunday 13 August
## Psalm 105

# Count your blessings

## PREPARE

Today's title might have reminded you of an old hymn and the ending of its chorus: 'And it will surprise you what the Lord hath done.'* What has the Lord done in your life that surprised you?

. . . . . . . . . . . . . . . . . . . . . . . . . . . . . . . . . . . . . . . . . . . . . . . . . . . . . . . . . . .

## READ
**Psalm 105**

## EXPLORE

This psalm and next Sunday's are considered to be 'companion psalms', both having a lot of detail about the history of the Hebrews, in which we are immersed on weekdays. This one is full of praise for all the Lord has done for his chosen people. It begins with extolling the Lord and encouraging its hearers to praise him (vs 1–7) – and that includes a reminder of exactly who they are (v 6).

This is followed by a discourse of the Hebrews' early history – reflecting and amplifying much of Hebrews 11 – and is notable for its focus on the deeds of the Lord. Look through from verse 8 and count the number of things the Lord has done – all those actions on behalf of his people.

The reason for all of this is in the final verse, and it reminds us that there is purpose and intention with all God's

actions (Hebrews 9:14). They're not a whim or conducted randomly. In this case, he did all he did in order that he would be known and understood as a God worth following and obeying.

He remembers his covenant for ever, the promise he made, for a thousand generations.

**Psalm 105:8**

---

## RESPOND

Spend some time giving thanks to God for all he has done in your life. There might be surprising things – or equally, small everyday matters. All of them can inspire our commitment and obedience.

---

*Johnson Oatman (1856–1922), 'Count Your Blessings'

. . . . . . . . . . . . . . . . . . . . . . . . . . . . . . . . . . . . . . . . . . . . . . . . . . . . . . . . . . .

**Bible in a year:** Proverbs 11,12;  Colossians 3

# Fix your eyes

## PREPARE

If you're an archer, keeping your eyes on the target is key to hitting the bullseye. In fact, any project worth doing needs focus and determination. What are you currently focused on, spiritually? How's it going?

## READ

**Hebrews 10:11-25**

## EXPLORE

The first part of today's reading reinforces the theme of Saturday's (vs 11-18). We are reminded that because of Jesus' sacrifice (this is one of the author's 'therefore' moments: vs 19-21), there are three things we should be motivated to do.

First, to draw close to God. No sin or guilt is in the way any longer to stop us being at one with our heavenly Father (v 22). Secondly, to hang on tight and not waver in our hope. Not because of who we are, but because of who God is: he is faithful to his promises (v 23). And thirdly, to encourage one another. Encourage in love, encourage in doing good for others and encourage meeting together so that we support one another (vs 24,25). Hurray! How marvellous!

Sometimes, though, God feels far away. Sometimes I feel wobbly, faith-wise.

Sometimes I don't want to bother encouraging anyone. I have learned, and am still learning, that looking at Jesus and focusing on what he has done helps me. It sounds simple – and sometimes takes effort in itself – but it's always worth it. And it's part of being made holy (v 14).

> For by one sacrifice he has made perfect for ever those who are being made holy.

**Hebrews 10:14**

## RESPOND

Go back to 'Prepare' and think again about your spiritual focus. Ask God for the strength and help you need to keep your aim fixed and your hand steady.

**Bible in a year:** Proverbs 13,14; Colossians 4

## Tuesday 15 August
Hebrews 10:26–39

# Standing firm

## PREPARE
'On Christ, the solid rock, I stand; all other ground is sinking sand.'* When have you needed to be really aware of the rock under your feet?

........................................................................

## READ
**Hebrews 10:26–39**

## EXPLORE
The two sections in this passage each have a key word. In the first section, that word is 'deliberately' (v 26). The writer to the Hebrews is not talking about occasions when we might unwittingly or accidentally do something sinful. Neither is it about giving in to temptation or drifting away (however that may happen) from faith. Those things can be repented of and forgiven; people can be restored. The writer is talking about public, wilful, intentional denial of everything to do with Christ and his sacrifice, which was once believed. And that will, rightly, come under God's judgement (vs 29–31).

In the second section, the key word is 'persevere' (v 36). Readers are reminded of difficult things they've suffered, or times when they've been a support to others going through similar things. Perseverance is hard work; perseverance is gritted teeth, fists clenched, keeping on keeping on – but with the confidence that we're doing God's will, persevering by his Spirit and in his strength, and that his rich reward to the faithful will be ours (v 39; see also Romans 5:3–5).

So do not throw away your confidence; it will be richly rewarded.

**Hebrews 10:35**

## RESPOND
It is a great sadness to be aware of anyone who was once a person of clear faith repudiating it. It is a great joy to see someone persevering in faith through challenging times. Pray for anyone you know in either circumstance.

*Edward Mote (1797–1874)

........................................................................

**Bible in a year:** Proverbs 15,16;  1 Thessalonians 1

# Blessed assurance

## PREPARE

'I gotta have faith, faith, faith,' sang George Michael.* If you check out the lyrics, they're all about wanting something or someone better in the future. What do you have – or need – faith for?

## READ

**Hebrews 11:1–7**

## EXPLORE

So, we have arrived at Hebrews 11, this wonderful chapter detailing many Old Testament heroes, what they did and the faith they had. Today's reading contains three of the earliest: Abel, who made a proper, acceptable sacrifice to God; Enoch, who walked faithfully with God; and Noah, whose ark meant that the future God had planned could take place (see Genesis 4–9 for their stories).

The reading also reminds us that faith 'is our handle on what we can't see' (v 1, *The Message*). God's creative power is believed in by faith. Faith speaks into the future (v 4) and when we believe in God he is pleased (v 6). One thought, however: it's tempting to think that to please God our faith has to be of a magnitude like that of these characters. Jesus said even a mustard seed of faith can achieve great things (Luke 17:5,6);

and that's comforting to remember when, as I once heard a past SU National Director say, faith is sometimes like clinging on by your fingertips – and you bite your nails.

## ... without faith it is impossible to please God.

**Hebrews 11:6**

## RESPOND

If you feel your faith is only just clinging on today, remember that we please God even with a tiny amount of trust in him. Pray for anyone in those circumstances that the knowledge that God delights in our trust will encourage and bring confidence.

*George Michael, 'Faith', 1987

**Bible in a year:** Proverbs 17,18;  Psalm 91

# Thursday 17 August
## Hebrews 11:8–22

# Life after life

## PREPARE

At funerals or memorial services, there is a eulogy of some kind about the person who has died. The last one I heard made the congregation laugh quite a lot! What would you like to be remembered for?

## READ
**Hebrews 11:8–22**

## EXPLORE

Today we move on to the stories of those who (in some church traditions) are remembered on the first Sunday of Advent: the patriarchs. These are the founding family of all who call themselves Hebrews, and the faith family of all who through Jesus inherit the blessing given to Abraham (Galatians 3:14). It's astonishing to be reminded of what their faith in God led them to do: leave everything comfortable and familiar and set off without knowing the destination; have a child at a great age; believe in resurrection… And that's just the beginning!

Even at the point of death, these people were trusting that what they hoped for would one day come to pass (v 13). God made specific promises to Abraham about the future, which he believed. For us today, perhaps believing promises made by God for the future is, ultimately, all about death. For all who trust in Jesus, dying is the final step of faith. We live in faith and we die in faith, trusting that Jesus will meet us and take us home to the heavenly city, 'whose architect and builder is God' (v 10).

All these people were still living by faith when they died.

**Hebrews 11:13**

### RESPOND
Give thanks for those whose lives of faith have inspired you; pray for those approaching the end of life to have confidence and trust in God for the final step.

**Bible in a year:** Proverbs 19,20; 1 Thessalonians 2

# Major or minor?

## PREPARE
**What kind of ministry or service do you most admire? Why? What kind of ministry or service do you carry out? Why? Do those two questions have any connection?**

## READ
**Hebrews 11:23–31**

## EXPLORE
We move on in the history of the Hebrews to the story of Moses and the exit from Egypt. He has already been discussed by the author in chapter 3. Moses was called 'faithful as a servant in all God's house' (3:5). Not claiming any status for himself, and considering earthly riches of little comparative value, mark him out as someone looking to the future promise. The phrase that this was 'for the sake of Christ' indicates this (v 26).

There's also Joshua, who carried out God's instructions so that Jericho would fall (v 30). Both he and Moses had upfront, leadership roles in Israel's history. But the passage is topped and tailed by other people: first, Moses' parents (Amram and Jochebed, Exodus 6:20), whose faith prompted them to hide him from the Egyptian slaughter (v 23; Exodus 1:22 – 2:4); and lastly, Rahab, whose actions were significant in the conquest of Canaan (v 31). Their roles may have been less prominent (or you might think not...), but they are equally commended for their faith.

> ... he persevered because he saw him who is invisible.
>
> **Hebrews 11:27**

## RESPOND
I once heard someone say that God does not require success; he asks for our obedience. Whatever ministry God has called you to, whether it's seen by many or known to only a few, pray for the strength to remain faithful as you do it.

**Bible in a year:** Proverbs 21,22;  1 Thessalonians 3

# Connections

## PREPARE
**What has the greatest challenge to your faith been? What – and who – helped you to get through it? What was the outcome of the challenge, faith-wise?**

•••••••••••••••••••••••••••••••••••••••••••••••••••••••••••••••••••••••••••••

## READ
**Hebrews 11:32–40**

## EXPLORE
And finally... the writer of Hebrews takes us at a bit of a gallop through a list of Old Testament people whose lives evidenced great faith in God. There is also a list of events, which help us to identify a few more, such as Daniel and the three young men in the fiery furnace. Each of those people and events has much to teach us about what living a life of faith means and about what may happen as a result of doing so.

The whole of chapter 11 provides us with examples, big, small and unknown, of people whose lives demonstrated faith in God. For pretty much all of them, the circumstances in which they exhibited it were challenging, at the least – and for many, horrific. But all of them have their faith in God commended (v 39), and all of them are 'waiting for Christ's faithful people to join them'* (v 40). We are some of those people. We are some of those 'who through faith' (v 33)

have lived – and are living – through circumstances in which we put our trust in God and prove his faithfulness to us. We're connected by faith to them.

> ... who through faith...
>
> **Hebrews 11:33**

### RESPOND
Some of the descriptions in the passage of what happened to people make truly terrible reading. And for many Christians in some parts of the world, those things are still realities. Pray for them, that they are able to persevere too.

*H Marshall, S Travis and I Paul, *Exploring the New Testament, Volume 2*, London, SPCK, 2021

•••••••••••••••••••••••••••••••••••••••••••••••••••••••••••••••••••••••••••••

**Bible in a year:** Proverbs 23,24;  Psalms 92,93

# Heads – and tails

## PREPARE
'You took all my shame away, there defeated my sin; opened up the gates of heav'n and have beckoned me in.'* Echo verse 48 of the psalm for all God offers us through Christ.

## READ
**Psalm 106**

## EXPLORE
I wrote last Sunday that this and last week's psalms are companions – but really, they're more like two sides of the same coin. Last week's extolled the Lord's mighty acts for his people; this week we read, sadly, of the abject failure of the people to follow and obey.

The psalm writer openly acknowledges their sinfulness (v 6). It's not covered up or glossed over. Some of the words and phrases used are striking: 'gave no thought'; 'did not remember'; 'soon forgot'; 'despised'; 'grumbled'; 'aroused the Lord's anger'. There are more. It's a sorry tale of forgetfulness, ingratitude and rebellion. And of course, God was rightly angered (vs 40–43).

Yet look at the Lord's response in verses 44 to 46: 'heard'; 'remembered'; 'relented'. He allowed his people to suffer the consequences of their sin, but time after time, 'out of his great love', they were forgiven and restored. And that cycle continued until the blood of Christ opened a new and living way – for everyone. In the new covenant, God's grace, mercy and forgiveness are extended to all who will believe.

Yet he took note of their distress when he heard their cry.

**Psalm 106:44**

## RESPOND
Pray today for anyone you know who has forgotten God, who ignores or rejects the love he has for them. Ask the Lord to walk beside them, even though they may not recognise his presence, and pray for their return to knowing his love.

*Matt Redman, copyright © 1994, Thankyou Music

**Bible in a year:** Proverbs 25,26; 1 Thessalonians 4

## Monday 21 August
Hebrews 12:1–13

# Run the race

## PREPARE

**Talk to any competitive athlete, and they'll say that encouragement of the crowd is a major part of keeping going – and winning. The 2012 Olympics in London were a terrific example of that. Who encourages you in faith?**

·····························································

## READ

**Hebrews 12:1–13**

## EXPLORE

This passage begins and ends with athletic imagery. Like those we've been reading about in the last chapter, who finished their races and are now cheering us on, we too need to run and finish our own race (vs 1,2). Everything that impedes our feet should be discarded, and we need to be strong to keep going.

How? By training. The discipline we read of in verses 7 to 11 is to help us be fit for the race. Training for anything requires dedication and time, and, very often, pain and effort. We might not like it, but it'll get us where God calls us to be. It'll also help us develop into being those whose lives are right with God and at peace with him (v 11) – and that benefits both us and others.

Why? Because of Jesus. He's there at the centre of everything. He's our example of

how to run the race to the end, and how to endure so that God's purposes are accomplished. And not only is he with us by his Spirit as we run – encouraging and helping us when our spiritual feet are weary. He is there waiting to greet us when our race is done.

> Consider him who endured such opposition from sinners, so that you will not grow weary and lose heart.
>
> **Hebrews 12:3**

## RESPOND

How's your godly training going? How's your race progressing? Pray about wherever you're up to, for perseverance and encouragement.

·····························································

**Bible in a year:** Proverbs 27,28;  1 Thessalonians 5

# Worship and community

## PREPARE
Do you prefer a quiet, intimate setting, or a loud, exuberant gathering to worship? What do you dislike about ways of worshipping you can't so easily engage with?

. . . . . . . . . . . . . . . . . . . . . . . . . . . . . . . . . . . . . . . . . . . . . . . . . . . . . . . . . . . . . . . . . . . . . .

## READ
**Hebrews 12:14–29**

## EXPLORE
The first part of today's reading gives us an example of how *not* to live in community and harmony with others – that of Esau. The writer is concerned that the Hebrews do not lose out on the blessing that's rightly theirs. But it can be hard work being at peace with others and being holy. We need to 'make every effort' (v 14).

Then we move on to the description of what happened at Mount Sinai – the giving of the Law, amid the terrifying signs of God's presence and warnings not to approach (Exodus 19:12,13). That's followed by what Mount Zion is like – also filled with God's presence, but with open access to him through Jesus, who replaced the Law with the blood of the new covenant (vs 22–24). And as well as the heavenly hosts, there are also all the people who've run their race and now stand before God in perfect righteousness.

The final two verses remind us, however, that access to God is not to be taken lightly; he is the God of Mount Sinai *and* Mount Zion, so how we worship him matters (vs 28,29).

> … let us be thankful, and so worship God acceptably with reverence and awe.
>
> **Hebrews 12:28**

## RESPOND
What impact might the way we view God, and the way we worship him, have on how we engage with others? Is there, or should there be, a connection between those things? Think and pray about that today.

. . . . . . . . . . . . . . . . . . . . . . . . . . . . . . . . . . . . . . . . . . . . . . . . . . . . . . . . . . . . . . . . . . . . . .

**Bible in a year:** Proverbs 29,30;  2 Thessalonians 1

# Wednesday 23 August

Hebrews 13:1–16

# The heart of life

## PREPARE

Try to work out how much time you spend on different aspects of your life: faith life, family life, church life, leisure life and work life. What overlap is there between any of those?

. . . . . . . . . . . . . . . . . . . . . . . . . . . . . . . . . . . . . . . . . . . . . . . . . . . . . . . . . . . . .

## READ

**Hebrews 13:1–16**

## EXPLORE

Jesus is at the centre of this passage. We see glimpses of and read prophetic words about Jesus in the Old Testament. His sacrifice was prefigured by the old covenantal sacrifices made by the high priests. That's yesterday. Today, we can meet him and know him, love and serve him because of his sacrifice; and one day, we'll meet him face to face – for ever. The same Jesus, through the whole of time.

Because of Jesus, the way we live in relationship with others is important. Our fellow believers need loving (v 1) with his love. Those we don't know need his welcome and generosity (v 2). Those in trouble or struggling need his compassion (v 3). Our family lives and our personal lives should show his purity and integrity (vs 4,5). Those with spiritual authority should be honoured as Christ himself should be (v 7). We also need God's grace to stay on track (v 9).

Living like that is summed up in verses 15 and 16. While describing it as a sacrifice means it isn't necessarily easy, it pleases God.

> … let us continually offer to God a sacrifice of praise – the fruit of lips that openly profess his name.
>
> **Hebrews 13:15**

## RESPOND

How does it make you feel, to know that the way we live as Jesus' followers can please him – or not please him? Are there areas in your life where Jesus needs to be more central than he is? Pray about it.

. . . . . . . . . . . . . . . . . . . . . . . . . . . . . . . . . . . . . . . . . . . . . . . . . . . . . . . . . . . . .

**Bible in a year:** Proverbs 31;  Psalm 94

# One more thing...

## PREPARE
**Prayers of blessing occur throughout Scripture, and the contents are varied! What prayer of blessing would you pray for a group of people you wanted to encourage?**

. . . . . . . . . . . . . . . . . . . . . . . . . . . . . . . . . . . . . . . . . . . . . . . . . . . . . . . .

## READ
**Hebrews 13:17–25**

## EXPLORE
Now that the author of Hebrews has got the weighty matters down, it's as if he gets to other things they need to hear before the letter is ended. The final remarks of the writer might almost seem amusing (v 22 – really!) and are encouraging. They bring good news and greetings (vs 23,24) and connect with verses 17 to 19.

The sincere prayer of blessing the writer gives his readers (vs 20,21) sums up much of what we've been considering in the past couple of weeks: look at what has been accomplished by God in and through the new covenant established through Jesus Christ; and may the same God give you all you need to live and work for him. You can imagine the writer typing these words in bold, in italics and underlining them!

This blessing reminds the readers again that at the heart of everything, and overarching everything, is Jesus. In the very final sentence, we hear the writer offering all that God wants us to know and to have in and through all that Jesus has done: grace (v 25). How fitting a conclusion.

> ... may he work in us what is pleasing to him, through Jesus Christ, to whom be glory for ever and ever. Amen.
>
> **Hebrews 13:21**

## RESPOND
Use the blessing in verses 20 and 21 to pray for your church leaders, those in ministry who you know and care for, and for yourself – so that glory goes to the Lord as we seek to serve him and grow to be like him.

. . . . . . . . . . . . . . . . . . . . . . . . . . . . . . . . . . . . . . . . . . . . . . . . . . . . . . . .

**Bible in a year:** Ecclesiastes 1–3;  2 Thessalonians 2

# The slippery slope

**About the writer**
**Penny Boshoff**

Penny spends half the year in Dubai with her husband, Andrew, where she teaches, writes and relishes sharing the good news with people from around the world. Penny currently serves as President for SU Council (E&W).

Writers of historical accounts of nations select events and facts to build a picture of the past and to better understand the present. The writer of 1 and 2 Kings (let's call him the chronicler) unravels the past to understand the slippery slope of Israel's decline. His account explores the factors that led to Israel's eventual annihilation by Assyria. His history helps to explain why the people of Judah ended up as exiles in Babylon. If we want a forensic account of the domestic and foreign policies of Israel's kings, then the chronicler suggests we read 'the annals of the kings of Israel' which are, sadly, 'out of print'! His aim is altogether different.

The chronicler evaluates each of the kings of Israel and Judah through the lens of their covenant with the Lord God. His assessment is based on three main criteria: whether they worshipped the Lord alone, whether the king led God's people in keeping the covenant and whether they ruled justly and in accordance with God's law,

As the nation splits in two, the chronicler jumps between Israel and Judah, and the reigns of the kings overlap. It can be a dizzying read! If you are getting bogged down, take a step back and look for evidence of covenant-keeping in each chapter. Look also for the thread of hope which runs through our readings. Despite his people's unfaithfulness, God remains faithful and just. He keeps his covenant promises!

# First day at work

## PREPARE
**Pray: Father God, speak through your Word. Transform my thinking. Fill me with wisdom and discernment. Give me a humble and steadfast heart. Amen.**

## READ
**1 Kings 12:1–24**

## EXPLORE
God had already determined that Solomon's failure to rid Israel of idolatry would bring into play the consequences for breaking the covenant (see 1 Kings 11:11–13). God's word of judgement to Solomon and his word to Jeroboam (1 Kings 11:31–39) unfold through court politics following Solomon's death.

For all his legendary wisdom, Solomon had not modelled servant leadership but had become preoccupied with the trappings of kingship (see 1 Kings 10). The people had paid a harsh price for their king, just as the prophet Samuel said they would (v 4; see 1 Samuel 8:11–18). Solomon's magnificent projects were built with conscripted labour (eg 1 Kings 5:13–18), and his court and extensive administration were fed by a tax, paid in kind (1 Kings 4:7,27).

As the new ruler, Rehoboam has an opportunity to rule according to God's Word, as a servant king (v 7). Sadly, he lacked the humility and discernment to heed godly advice. The sense of entitlement evident in Rehoboam's generation (vs 10,11) was formed under Solomon's reign! Even as Rehoboam imitates his father's foolishness (with dire consequences, vs 16–21), we see God acting in mercy (vs 22–24). Do we recognise God's mercy in his discipline? Do we take heed when he disciplines us (v 24)?

'This is what the LORD says: do not go up to fight against your brothers, the Israelites. Go home, every one of you, for this is my doing.'
**1 Kings 12:24**

## RESPOND
Pause and consider: are you modelling a Christ-shaped life of service? Are your decisions based on God's Word or the opinions of your peers?

**Bible in a year:** Ecclesiastes 4,5;  2 Thessalonians 3

## Saturday 26 August
1 Kings 12:25 – 13:10

# Which voice to heed?

## PREPARE
'One thing God has spoken, two things I have heard: "Power belongs to you, God, and with you, Lord, is unfailing love"' (Psalm 62:11,12). How have you experienced God's power and his love? Praise him.

........................................................

## READ
**1 Kings 12:25 – 13:10**

## EXPLORE
In the thick of life, whose voice do we listen to? God had given Jeroboam a clear word and great promises (1 Kings 11:37–39), but Jeroboam chose to trust human wisdom instead – his own (v 26) and others' (v 28). His actions – fortifying cities (v 25), shoring up power and influence through religion (v 28) – were rooted in fear, not faith (v 27).

Jeroboam tries to build the nation himself by mimicking the forms of worship God had set up through Moses: priests, places of worship and festivals. None of it is done according to the Lord's command; it is all of Jeroboam's 'own choosing' (vs 31,32). It has the *form* of worship but not the heart. True devotion to God starts with obedience to his Word, as Jesus himself said: 'Anyone who loves me will obey my teaching. My Father will love them, and we will come to them and make our home with them' (John 14:23).

In love and power, God intervenes. By sending warning (13:2,3) and preventing Jeroboam from further sin at that moment (13:4–6), God shows him mercy and grace (v 6).

'This is what the LORD says: do not go up to fight against your brothers, the Israelites. Go home...' So they obeyed the word of the LORD...

**1 Kings 12:24**

---

## RESPOND
Pray the words of Psalm 139:23,24. Allow the Holy Spirit to show you where you may be rebelling against his Word. Turn back to God and ask for his help and strength to obey.

........................................................

**Bible in a year:** Ecclesiastes 6,7;  Psalms 95,96

# God's megaphone

## PREPARE
'Shall we accept good from God, and not trouble?' (Job 2:10). Think of a time you faced adversity. Did you share Job's outlook? How did the Lord meet you in your trouble?

.........................................................................

## READ
**Psalm 107**

## EXPLORE
Psalm 107 is a song of redemption stories. Four of the stanzas present case studies of people in dire need of rescue. Whether it is the suffering of the rootless and refugee (vs 4,5), the God-inflicted or self-inflicted suffering of those who rebel against God (vs 10–12,17,18,33,34) or those caught up in natural disasters (vs 23–27), discomfort and suffering can wake us up to our need for God. God, in his wisdom, may use adversity for our good (v 39).

As CS Lewis wrote, pain can be God's 'megaphone to rouse a deaf world'.* Look at the pivotal central verse in each stanza (vs 6,13,19,28). Although God is poised to intervene, he does not force his rescue on the unwilling. The moment someone cries out to him, his rescue is immediate and complete: he leads the refugee *straight* to a new city (v 7); he *cuts through* the hardest of chains (v 14). He is not only swift to rescue us from danger, disaster, darkness and death, he has a plan to bless us. He longs for us to be free (v 14), whole (v 20) and safe (vs 30,36).

Let the one who is wise heed these things and ponder the loving deeds of the LORD.
**Psalm 107:43**

## RESPOND
Depending on your circumstances, today may be a day for crying out to the Lord, or a day of giving thanks to him for his unfailing love.

*CS Lewis, *The Problem of Pain*, 1940

.........................................................................

**Bible in a year:** Ecclesiastes 8,9; 1 Timothy 1

## Monday 28 August
1 Kings 13:11–34

# Mysterious grace

## PREPARE
Peter spoke of the devil prowling around 'like a roaring lion looking for someone to devour' (1 Peter 5:8). Pray that you will be alert and ready to resist his attacks today.

## READ
**1 Kings 13:11–34**

## EXPLORE
What a disquieting end to the story! Having been the messenger and means of God's grace (v 6), and having resisted temptation (vs 8–10), the man of God is derailed by a false prophet (v 18; see Matthew 7:15)! Yet through his failure we trace the mysterious grace of God. The false prophet goes from being an instrument of Satan (the father of lies) to being a mouthpiece for the true Word of God (v 20).

The consequences of disobedience (v 24) become a sign confirming the truth of God's Word. The unexpected upshot is a conversion. As he aligns himself in death with the man of God from Judah, the old prophet is accepting God's Word against the place where he once worshipped (vs 11,32), and identifying with the place of true worship: Judah.

We too align ourselves in death with God's truly obedient man of God from Judah – Jesus Christ! As Romans 6:4 says, 'We were therefore buried with him through baptism into death in order that, just as Christ was raised from the dead through the glory of the Father, we too may live a new life.'

> 'When I die, bury me in the grave where the man of God is buried; lay my bones beside his bones.'
>
> **1 Kings 13:31**

## RESPOND
Pray that you and all God's people might hold firm and obey God's Word. Pray for those who oppose God, to hear the true Word and receive God's grace.

**Bible in a year:** Ecclesiastes 10,11; 1 Timothy 2

# The weight of leadership

## PREPARE

'Against you, you only, have I sinned and done what is evil in your sight; so you are right in your verdict and justified when you judge' (Psalm 51:4). What sin is the Holy Spirit bringing to your attention today?

## READ
**1 Kings 14:1–31**

## EXPLORE

Israel's clear purpose was to honour the God who had rescued them (Exodus 20:1–7; 2 Samuel 7:23; Deuteronomy 8:10,11). The king was to lead by example, honouring and obeying God alone, as David had done (v 8). Sadly, Jeroboam and Rehoboam fell short. The root cause of their failure as kings of Israel and Judah was idolatry (vs 9,22,23).

God had forewarned his people of the consequences of rebellion and idolatry (Deuteronomy 28). With the death of his son (vs 10,11), Jeroboam's dynasty would be short-lived. Through Ahijah's message, we see that God is right and fair in judgement. The boy would die but his burial meant he wasn't included in the curse (vs 12,13; see also Deuteronomy 28:26).

God's judgement on Judah's idolatry (vs 22–24), under Rehoboam's leadership, comes in the form of instability, insecurity, foreign incursions and rumbling civil war. The glories of Solomon's reign (v 26) have evaporated. Judah is now a vulnerable two-tribe state (Judah and Benjamin; see 12:21–23). Perhaps the mention of Rehoboam's Ammonite mother (vs 21,31) hints that the seeds of Rehoboam's failure were sown by his father, Solomon.

> You have made for yourself other gods, idols made of metal; you have aroused my anger and turned your back on me.
>
> **1 Kings 14:9**

---

## RESPOND

Pray for those in authority that they will heed God's Word, so that those they lead might live 'in all godliness and holiness' (1 Timothy 2:1,2).

---

**Bible in a year:** Ecclesiastes 12; 1 Timothy 3

## Wednesday 30 August
1 Kings 15:1–32

# Where lies your heart?

## PREPARE
**What or who motivates you? Where lies your heart? If you are not sure, try answering this question: What or who do you speak about with passion?**

## READ
**1 Kings 15:1–32**

## EXPLORE
The books of 1 and 2 Kings were written to explore the spiritual decline of God's people and why they were eventually taken captive to Assyria and Babylon. The spiritual health of a community begins in the heart of each individual and finds expression in our words and actions. Who or what we love determines what we talk about, how we prioritise our time and how we spend our money.

Here we have a spiritual health check of Abijah (v 3) and his son Asa (vs 11,14). Admittedly, Abijah had poor parental role models (vs 2,13), but he is still responsible for his own relationship with God. Asa, in contrast, put God's honour before family ties and influence (v 13). What each man is devoted to in his heart comes out in action, or lack of it! Although Abijah honours God in part (v 15), he does nothing to stamp out Judah's idolatry. Asa, in contrast, puts his faith into action (vs 11–15).

His God-centred life results in practical wisdom bringing blessing and security to the community (vs 17–22; see also Proverbs 9:10): Israel's King Baasha is forced to move his army north, saving Judah from the rumbling civil war (v 6; see also 1 Kings 12:24).

> Although he did not remove the high places, Asa's heart was fully committed to the LORD all his life.
>
> **1 Kings 15:14**

## RESPOND
What may need to move, or be torn down, to allow the Lord to be first in your heart?

---

**Bible in a year:** Song of Songs 1,2; Psalms 97,98

# A life's legacy

## PREPARE
If someone were to review your life so far, what would your legacy be?

...........................................................................................

## READ
**1 Kings 15:33 – 16:34**

## EXPLORE
When the people of Israel and Judah were exiled by Assyria and Babylon, those trying to make sense of events looked back to see where things went wrong. Throughout 1 and 2 Kings, the chronicler presents evidence clearly demonstrating how Israel and Judah had rejected God and aroused his anger.

When a leader resigns or dies, almost immediately there are articles assessing their 'legacy', as we saw when Queen Elizabeth died last year. Here, each king receives an assessment of their spiritual legacy! For these kings it is a dismal and worsening refrain (15:34; 16:2,7,13,19). In contrast to Asa's God-centred rule (15:33; 16:8), the kings of Israel rejected God. They chose to uphold, promote and reinforce the 'tradition' of idolatry established under Jeroboam. By the reign of Ahab we reach the nadir of evil (v 30), with the king of Israel blatantly rejecting the Lord to worship Baal and Asherah.

As this litany of idolatry, assassinations, plots and power struggles unfolds, we may be wondering where God is. The chronicler reminds us that God knows all, sees all and speaks into the darkest of situations (15:34; 16:1,7,12,34). Nothing, not even the most wicked regime, can stop God working.

'I lifted you up ... but you followed the ways of Jeroboam and caused my people Israel to sin and to arouse my anger by their sins.'
**1 Kings 16:2**

## RESPOND
Listen to the Taizé song, 'Within our darkest night'.* Pray for nations where the knowledge of God and of his Son, Jesus Christ, is being stamped out.

*https://www.youtube.com/watch?v=EqQsZK57OX8

...........................................................................................

**Bible in a year:** Song of Songs 3,4; 1 Timothy 4

## Friday 1 September
1 Kings 17:1–24

# Into darkness, God speaks

## PREPARE
Pray: Sanctify us, Lord, through your Word (see John 17:17). Help us today to live according to the truth, the living Word, that you have made known. Amen.

## READ
**1 Kings 17:1–24**

## EXPLORE
Into the darkness of Ahab's evil reign, God sends his messenger (v 1). But how do we know that this man, defined only by his place of birth, is a true prophet? The chronicler carefully places the fulfilment of God's Word through Joshua (16:34) next to the first words spoken by this unknown man from Tishbe (v 1). And he ends the chapter with a declaration of Elijah's credentials from an unlikely source: a foreign widow (v 24). The chronicler wants us to understand that Elijah is a true prophet: he hears God clearly and correctly. What he says comes true (see Deuteronomy 18:21,22).

Though drought and consequent famine are signs of God's judgement on his people's rebellion (v 1; see also Deuteronomy 28:15,20,22–24), God remains true to his covenant, providing protection and provision from unexpected sources for those who honour and obey him (vs 5,6,9). The shock for the original readers is that God's Word, his grace and his blessing extend beyond Israel's borders (v 9; see also Luke 4:24–27) to reach those who do not yet know him.

'Now I know that you are a man of God and that the word of the LORD from your mouth is the truth.'

**1 Kings 17:24**

## RESPOND
God directed events to meet the needs of Elijah and the widow. Who might he be using to meet your need today? And who might he be bringing across your path, to meet the living God and experience his blessing and care?

**Bible in a year:** Song of Songs 5,6;  1 Timothy 5

# Time to speak out

## PREPARE
'Rulers persecute me without cause, but my heart trembles at your word' (Psalm 119:161). Pray: Lord, give me a listening heart as you speak through your Word. Amen.

## READ
**1 Kings 18:1–19**

## EXPLORE
It takes courage to follow God in a culture where everything except God is worshipped (v 12). It takes perseverance to keep your heart and mind focused on the Lord when your workplace is hostile to God (v 13). It takes wisdom and discernment to know when to do what is right 'behind the scenes' (v 4) and when to speak out (v 16). But it is not easy! For Obadiah every day was a battle between faith and fear.

Elijah's 'chance' meeting with Obadiah (vs 1,2,7) is, of course, a God-incidence. As Ahab's official, Obadiah's duty was to arrest the nation's most wanted man. Through Elijah's request God tests Obadiah's loyalty, challenging him to make a choice. Is his priority God (and God's prophet)? Or his earthly boss, King Ahab? Will he live by faith or fear (vs 9,14)?

For most of us, speaking up for God's truth may not be a matter of life or death, but it may cost us a promotion, a relationship or our reputation. The question for Obadiah that day, as it is for each of us every day, is what is more important: my job, relationship, reputation, life… or God and his Word?

'If I go and tell Ahab and he doesn't find you, he will kill me. Yet I your servant have worshipped the LORD since my youth.'
**1 Kings 18:12**

### RESPOND
How is the Holy Spirit challenging you? Is he asking you to speak out where previously you have been silent?

**Bible in a year:** Song of Songs 7,8; Psalms 99–101

## Sunday 3 September
Psalm 108

# Questions of praise

## PREPARE
**Start with a song of praise, such as 'Great is thy faithfulness'\* or 'To God be the glory'.\*\***

........................................................................................

## READ
**Psalm 108**

## EXPLORE
Psalm 108 answers some key questions about praise:

*How* should we praise? We are to be determined, unwavering and wholehearted (v 1) in praise. That means that we can praise God for who he is and what he has done even when we are sad or hard-pressed.

*When* should we praise? At the beginning of every new day (v 2) before we do anything else! And when we face trouble (vs 6,12) and uncertainty (v 11). Notice how David is plagued with doubt about whether God will go with him into battle (v 11), but he reacts to uncertainty by praising God.

*Where* should we praise? David praises God among people who don't know or acknowledge the Lord (v 3). There's a challenge for us! Singing worship songs at work may not be appropriate, but honouring God and speaking warmly of what he means to us definitely is!

*Why* should we praise? Because God's love is boundless. He is committed to saving, helping and blessing us (vs 4,6). And he is in control. Everything and everyone is under his rule (vs 8,9). That includes those who acknowledge him (Gilead, Manasseh, Ephraim and Judah) and those who don't (Moab, Edom and Philistia).

Be exalted, O God, above the heavens; let your glory be over all the earth.
**Psalm 108:5**

---

## RESPOND
Whatever doubt or difficulty you are facing, hold on to God. Call out to him. Praise him, because with him, there is always hope (v 13).

---

\*Thomas Chisholm, 1923
\*\*Fanny Crosby, 1875

........................................................................................

**Bible in a year:** Isaiah 1,2;  1 Timothy 6

# Israel's influencers

## PREPARE
Who or what is king of your heart? What voices shape your thoughts and influence your actions?

· · · · · · · · · · · · · · · · · · · · · · · · · · · · · · · · · · · · · · · · · · · · · · ·

## READ
**1 Kings 18:20–46**

## EXPLORE
Ancient Israel did not have social media, but they did have influencers. The first influencer, Jeroboam, encouraged the nation to dilute their worship of the Lord (1 Kings 12:28–33). Ahab and Jezebel actively promoted worship of the Canaanite gods of rain and fertility: Baal and Asherah (1 Kings 16:30–33).

Through his challenge and deliberate actions, Elijah makes it clear that only one God can be worshipped, and that worship was to be done God's way – at the place God had chosen (v 30) and at God's time (v 36). When the fire fell, it was proof of God's power and his jealous anger (vs 36–38). Not only is the sodden sacrifice consumed, but also the 12 altar stones (representing Israel), the earth itself and even the water (a clear poke in the eye for the rain god, Baal!). In God's mercy his judgement fell on the sacrifice, not the people. In the same way, on the cross, God's wrath fell not on us but on Jesus.

Fire from heaven lighting sodden wood is impressive, but the real miracle is people turning back to the living God in worship and obedience (v 39). And when they do, God pours down blessing according to his covenant promise (vs 41,45; see Deuteronomy 11:13–15).

> When all the people saw this, they fell prostrate and cried, 'The LORD – he is God! The LORD – he is God!'

**1 Kings 18:39**

## RESPOND
The people's reaction was immediate and appropriate. What might you need to get rid of, or turn away from, so that you can worship the Lord wholeheartedly?

· · · · · · · · · · · · · · · · · · · · · · · · · · · · · · · · · · · · · · · · · · · · · · ·

**Bible in a year:** Isaiah 3–5;  2 Timothy 1

# Tuesday 5 September

1 Kings 19:1–21

# God's gentle word

## PREPARE

'Be still, and know that I am God' (Psalm 46:10). Stillness takes practice! Begin your practice now.

• • • • • • • • • • • • • • • • • • • • • • • • • • • • • • • • • • • • • • • • • • • • • • • • •

## READ

**1 Kings 19:1–21**

## EXPLORE

The adrenaline from the Mount Carmel success has dissipated. Elijah is fearful, depleted and focused on his own situation (vs 4,10). It is a reminder that God's messengers are human. Like us, they have limitations, weaknesses and flaws (see James 5:17,18; Psalm 103:13,14). Most of us have had (or will have) moments of wanting to run and hide from hostility and the pressures of life. Notice how the Lord deals with Elijah's physical need for rest, food and safety (vs 5–8) first. Only then does he tackle Elijah's mental and spiritual state.

Elijah seems stuck with the wrong notion that he is the only one upholding God's honour (vs 10,14). He has forgotten Obadiah and the turnaround at Mount Carmel (18:39,40). God is in the business of renewing our minds (Romans 12:2), but that can only happen when we focus our attention on him (v 11) and not ourselves. The powerful forces of nature were signs of the ancient gods, but the true God who created all reveals himself through words – quiet words (v 12) – words that reminded Elijah that God is in control and that gave Elijah a renewed purpose.

## And after the fire came a gentle whisper.

**1 Kings 19:12**

## RESPOND

Have you considered a 'holy day' with God? Take some time, away from other distractions, to let him refresh you and reshape your view of him and of yourself.

• • • • • • • • • • • • • • • • • • • • • • • • • • • • • • • • • • • • • • • • • • • • • • • • •

**Bible in a year:** Isaiah 6,7; 2 Timothy 2

# An antidote for arrogance

## PREPARE

'You are my refuge and my shield; I have put my hope in your word' (Psalm 119:114). If you are feeling embattled today, picture God standing between you and whatever it is that threatens you.

## READ

**1 Kings 20:1–21**

## EXPLORE

With a coalition of 32 kings of city states, Ben-Hadad was supremely confident that he would get whatever he wanted. Verses 2 to 12 are a chilling example of the way a powerful nation with many allies plays at diplomacy, increasing their demands until war is inevitable. What happened in 850 BC happens still today!

Even though Ahab did not seek God in this national moment of crisis, God in his mercy sends a messenger. God uses this as a teaching moment for Ahab (v 13). God could have struck the Aramean army down with a word, but he chooses to involve Ahab and his army. And that meant that Ahab had to listen and obey.

God still does the impossible, bringing about change and justice by working through those who will obey his call. We are prone to taking the credit rather than giving God the glory. Maybe that is why God is so specific about the battle (vs 13,14). It is not skill or experience that matters, but the power of God at work as the people obey (vs 19–21).

'Do you see this vast army? I will give it into your hand today, and then you will know that I am the LORD.'

**1 Kings 20:13**

## RESPOND

Are you facing a situation that appears overwhelming? Ask the Lord for his perspective on your situation, for wisdom on the steps you need to take next and for the determination to obey.

**Bible in a year:** Isaiah 8,9; Psalm 102

# Misconceptions

## PREPARE

Pray: Heavenly Father, by the power of your Holy Spirit, speak to me through your Word, put right my wrong thinking and set me on your path of life. Amen.

......................................................................

## READ

**1 Kings 20:22–33**

## EXPLORE

This passage deals with key misconceptions about the God of Israel: that he is limited (v 23) and that his mercy means he is a pushover (v 31).

The Arameans, like other ancient peoples, believed in gods with limited power who only had jurisdiction over distinct geographical areas. The Lord wants Ahab to think differently (v 28). The Lord is not limited; he is not even in a battle with any other god. There is no contest because no other gods exist! He proves this by using Israel's paltry army (v 27) to inflict heavy losses on a well-equipped force that vastly outnumbered them. The writer of 1 and 2 Kings implies that God controls every event in this battle, even the freak 'accident' (v 30).

The second misconception is the nature of God's mercy. Ben-Hadad assumed that his life came at the price of a city or two (v 34). But rebellion against God has only one outcome: death (v 42). Ahab paid the price for the mercy shown to Ben-Hadad, just as another king, Jesus, paid the price for the mercy shown to us. His life for our life.

'Because the Arameans think the LORD is a god of the hills and not a god of the valleys, I will deliver this vast army into your hands, and you will know that I am the LORD.'

**1 Kings 20:28**

---

## RESPOND

Pray: Heavenly Father, you are unlimited in power. We praise you! Lord Jesus Christ, you gave your life as a ransom for ours. We praise you! Holy Spirit, you show us the glories of God. We praise you!

....................................................................

**Bible in a year:** Isaiah 10–12;  2 Timothy 3

# Integrity

## PREPARE

'Search me, God, and know my heart … See if there is any offensive way in me, and lead me in the way everlasting' (Psalm 139:23,24).

. . . . . . . . . . . . . . . . . . . . . . . . . . . . . . . . . . . . . . . . . . . . . . . . . . . . . . . . . . .

## READ

**1 Kings 21:1–29**

## EXPLORE

Our response to God's discipline matters. Do we gladly submit or do we brood? Ahab's default response was to sulk (20:43; 21:4). How do we react when we don't get what we want? Do we reason and bargain? Do we find subtle ways of doing what we want anyway?

Look at Ahab's recounting of the discussion with Naboth. Notice how he leaves out the part that really grated with him: God's clear instruction about land inheritance (vs 3,4,6). Honouring God means obeying what he has said – even the bits that don't suit us!

Jezebel and Ahab have disobeyed the first commandment to worship God alone, so they have no qualms in breaking the rest: coveting, lying, murdering and stealing (vs 2,8,13,16). And worse, they lead others astray (vs 11–13; see also Mark 9:42).

God expects his people to live lives of integrity and godliness in private as well as in public. When we fail (which we will), are we quick to repent (v 27)? God responds to those who are lowly and contrite in heart and who tremble at his Word (v 29, see also Isaiah 66:2).

'This is what the LORD says: have you not murdered a man and seized his property?'

**1 Kings 21:19**

## RESPOND

In what ways have you been looking to get your own way? Be honest with the Lord about the parts of his Word that grate with you. Ask him to transform your mind and soften your heart.

. . . . . . . . . . . . . . . . . . . . . . . . . . . . . . . . . . . . . . . . . . . . . . . . . . . . . . . . . . .

**Bible in a year:** Isaiah 13,14;  2 Timothy 4

## Saturday 9 September
1 Kings 22:1–28

# Speaking truth to power

## PREPARE
**Pray:** Heavenly Father, as I come to you, source of all truth, prepare my heart and mind to hear your Word to me today.

. . . . . . . . . . . . . . . . . . . . . . . . . . . . . . . . . . . . . . . . . . . . . . . . . . . . . . . . . . . . .

## READ
**1 Kings 22:1–28**

## EXPLORE

Despite his outward repentance (21:27–29), Ahab was unchanged. He is supposed to be leading the nation in honouring God, but he doesn't even seek God's direction in his day-to-day work! And when prompted by Judah's king to consult the Lord, he goes to the prophets of the wrong god! The 450 prophets mentioned here may well have been the prophets of Asherah (1 Kings 18:19). Their prophecy (v 6) is generic, with no mention of Israel's God, which is why Jehoshaphat intervenes again (v 7). Could you be a 'Jehoshaphat' for someone today? If someone has a problem or decision, encourage them to seek God. And gently redirect them if they are going to the wrong place!

1 Kings 22 illustrates the sticky problem of truth and leadership. Too often, leaders surround themselves with advisers who tell them what they want to hear. Those who question or present uncomfortable truths may be branded troublemakers (v 8; 18:17) and find themselves without a job, or worse (vs 26,27).

Ahab has failed to understand that God is in control (vs 19–23). The scene is reminiscent of Job, chapters 1 and 2. While Job remains true to God, despite temptation, Ahab continues rejecting God's truth and listening to lies.

'As surely as the LORD lives, I can only tell him what the LORD tells me.'

**1 Kings 22:14**

---

### RESPOND
Pray the words of Philippians 1:9–11 for leaders in church, government and businesses. Pray too for Christians to speak God's truth to those in leadership.

---

**Bible in a year:** Isaiah 15,16;  Psalm 103

# Song of the wounded

## PREPARE

**Pray: Lord God, you understand our every desire and every thought. You know us completely and you still want us to draw close to you. Thank you.**

## READ

**Psalm 109**

## EXPLORE

I am glad David wrote Psalm 109. Trace the emotions that lie behind David's words. It is reassuring to know we can be completely open with God about what we are going through and how we feel about it. Do you have a complaint? Are you indignant? Take those feelings to God (vs 2–5). Are you desperate (vs 1,6,21,26), hurt and at the end of your resources (vs 22–25)? Pour it out to the Lord. Are you fuming about injustice (vs 16–18), and inwardly boiling for revenge (vs 8–15)? Release your frustration, your anger and your darkest desires to God. He can handle it.

When we bring our darkest thoughts into God's light through prayer, something shifts. Prayer is the ultimate safe space to release our dark thoughts and emotions. God does not leave us stewing in our darkness. Notice how David's rant of verses 7 to 20 and the self-absorption of verses 21 to 25 change to something more measured by the last stanza.

Through prayer, God shifts our focus to his character. Once we are assured of God's love (v 26), his justice (v 31) and his willingness to bless (v 28), we can leave our grievances with him, knowing he will do what is good and right.

While they curse, may you bless; may those who attack me be put to shame, but may your servant rejoice.

**Psalm 109:28**

## RESPOND

God knows you and your present situation completely. Pour out your heart to him.

**Bible in a year:** Isaiah 17–20;  Titus 1

# Monday 11 September

1 Kings 22:29–53

# A tale of two kings

## PREPARE

'I have hidden your word in my heart that I may not sin against you' (Psalm 119:11). How does God's Word find its way into your heart? How do you carry his Word with you through the day?

.........................................................................

## READ

**1 Kings 22:29–53**

## EXPLORE

Ahab now has enough information to make a good decision (22:19–23), but he chooses not to heed God's Word (v 29). It is almost laughable to see Ahab's attempts to outwit God (v 30). But when God decides to enact judgement (v 34), nothing will hinder him.

God's judgement is not a topic that most people want to discuss or even think about. How might people today attempt to get round God's judgement? Jesus was clear about judgement in Matthew 25:31,32 and in his vision to John (Revelation 20:11–15). He has given us enough information to make wise decisions.

While Ahab receives disaster and death, Jehoshaphat receives the mercy and protection of God (vs 32,33). What did Jehoshaphat's God-honouring reign (v 43) look like day to day? He sought God's counsel (22:5), he was discerning about advice (22:6,7), he encouraged others to seek God and rebuked ungodly conduct (22:8), he learned from past mistakes (vs 48,49; see v 4) and he was rigorous about holiness (v 46). Let's 'be more Jehoshaphat' today!

> In everything he followed the ways of his father Asa and did not stray from them; he did what was right in the eyes of the LORD.

**1 Kings 22:43**

## RESPOND

Pray: Heavenly Father, you whose hands formed me and made me – 'give me understanding to learn your commands. Teach me knowledge and good judgement, for I trust your commands'. Amen (from Psalm 119:73,66).

.........................................................................

**Bible in a year:** Isaiah 21,22;  Titus 2

# A legacy of love

............................

Could you leave a gift in your will and ensure
the good news of Jesus is shared with
generations to come?

'...we will tell the next generation the praiseworthy deeds of the Lord, his power, and
the wonders he has done.' **Psalm 78:4**

# The parables

## What is a parable?

Like all good preachers, Jesus made good use of stories. However, unlike modern preachers, Jesus' stories were not an introduction to longer teaching, but often the substance of the teaching itself. Parables might seem straightforward on the surface, but they require teasing out by Jesus' listeners.

A parable is a story that contains a deeper, perhaps subversive message. Jesus takes a point – such as what it means to be a neighbour (Luke 10:25–37) – and places it inside a story which enables alert listeners to form an answer for themselves. In the parable of the Good Samaritan Jesus ends by asking the lawyer, 'Which of these three do you think was a neighbour to the man who fell into the hands of robbers?' He does not bluntly tell the lawyer what to think; he asks him to draw his own conclusion. Often Jesus doesn't explain the parable, leaving his disciples puzzled (Mark 4:10–13) or his opponents discomforted (Mark 12:12).

## Why did Jesus teach through parables?

Teaching through storytelling and illustrations was a common method of teaching in the ancient world. As with any good sermon illustration, many of Jesus' parables tell stories of people (farmers, landlords, family relationships) that would be instantly recognisable to the listening crowd.

The Old Testament also has a few figurative stories in it. Isaiah 5:1–7 portrays Israel as God's vineyard, later picked up by Jesus in his parables (Matthew 20:1–16; Mark 12:1–12). The prophet Nathan tells King David, who has committed adultery, an emotive story about a poor farmer whose one lamb is snatched to feed the guests of a rich man (2 Samuel 12:1–6). When David expresses outrage, Nathan dramatically confronts him with the words: 'You are the man!'

Nathan's story gets through David's defences until he suddenly finds himself faced by God's judgement. Jesus' parables do something similar, whether they are about God's judgement or God's love.

The listeners find themselves confronted with an unexpected truth delivered in the form of a story. For a great example of this, read the three parables in Luke 15 and see how Jesus builds up his theme, eventually confronting the Pharisees in the person of the elder brother.

It is likely that Jesus has taken the prophetic tradition of Isaiah and Nathan and developed it into a style characteristic of his ministry. We read that he delighted the crowds with his storytelling, and it's not difficult to see why.

## What are the different styles of parable in the Gospels?

Parables appear in the synoptic Gospels (Matthew, Mark and Luke), but not in John. Their common features are that they tell a story, or at least describe a scene from which the listeners are to infer a truth about the kingdom of God. The parable of the sower appears in all three synoptics and is the keystone parable which introduces us to this method of Jesus' teaching.

Matthew and Luke contain parables unique to their particular Gospel. In Matthew we have the parables of the sheep and the goats and the ten bridesmaids, with their focus on coming judgement. In Luke we have the Good Samaritan and the prodigal son with their emphasis on the outcast. Some parables still present headaches to interpreters today. Read the parable of the unjust steward (or 'shrewd manager') in Luke 16:1–15, and see what you make of it!

## How should we read the parables?

Context in the Gospels is really important. When reading a parable, go back to the beginning of the section (this may be two or three parables earlier) and see who Jesus' listeners are. Are they the disciples, the crowds, the Pharisees, or a mixture of all of them? This will help you see whom Jesus is addressing.

Imagine yourself into the story – and not always into the most sympathetic character! For example, there are four main characters in the parable of the Good Samaritan. Why might they act as they do? How would you feel if you were in their shoes?

Allow the parable to challenge you, just as Jesus challenged his listeners. Most of us have something of the Pharisee within us. Be prepared to be shocked as you hear Jesus pointing out the times when your values may not be identical to those of God's kingdom.

**Writer: Toby Hole**

**Further resources:**
Paula Gooder, *The Parables*, Canterbury Press, 2020
NT Wright, *Matthew, Mark and Luke for Everyone*, SPCK, 2001

# The coming kingdom of God

About the writer
**Henry Cross**

Henry is married to Debra and they have four children and a very big dog! Henry and Debra lead The Rock and Redeemer Vineyard Church in Dunstable, Bedfordshire. When any spare time presents itself, he loves barbecuing, walking with his dog, reading, playing the guitar and meeting new people!

For anyone who has been following Jesus for any length of time, it's never far into that journey before you first hear the phrase 'the kingdom of God'. And when we hear it, it causes us to ask questions: What is this kingdom like? Where is this kingdom? How can I gain entry to it? And more besides.

The Gospel of Mark is not primarily concerned with giving an ordered account of Jesus' life and times – the writer leaves that to Luke and Matthew. But it is written to convey what becoming a disciple of Jesus, the King of this kingdom, requires of us ordinary, everyday women and men from all walks of life.

It is like a manifesto of the kingdom of God. Perhaps you have read a manifesto of a political party? They tend to be brochures which make bold claims about what life would be like if a particular political party got into power. Mark's Gospel is written to show its readers what the kingdom of God is and how it operates. And invariably, it's just as true now as it was for the people of Jesus' day – and often it isn't how we might imagine.

The Gospel of Mark is a foot-hard-down ride that takes us into the very heart of why Jesus came and what our response should be to that. So strap yourself in and prepare to be inspired and challenged by Jesus.

# Camel's hair and honey...

## PREPARE
As you quieten yourself before God, pray 'your kingdom come, your will be done, on earth as it is in heaven' (Matthew 6:10).

. . . . . . . . . . . . . . . . . . . . . . . . . . . . . . . . . . . . . . . . . . . . . . . . . . . . . . . . . . . . . . . . . .

## READ
**Mark 1:1-8**

## EXPLORE
The Jews of Jesus' time were awaiting the prophet Elijah's return to precede the coming of Messiah (vs 1-3; Malachi 4:5; see also Matthew 17:10-13). Every Passover supper they would leave a place set for him in the hope that he would return and announce Messiah's arrival (and the imminent end of Roman occupation). And here, stepping onto the scene, comes this unkempt and strange figure of John the Baptist – complete with locusts and honey stuck in his beard (v 6)!

The prophet Elijah is described as a hairy man with a leather belt around his waist (2 Kings 1:8), and for him, the Jordan River was a protective barrier from the murderous King Ahab during the drought that he prophesied (1 Kings 17:1,3). John the Baptist seems to fit the description of the longed-for messenger (vs 2,3)!

God's kingdom was moving, and John had been sent in the spirit of Elijah, as Jesus later confirms (Matthew 11:7-14). But many people missed it because he hadn't come as they expected. They were looking to the empty seats at Passover – and all the while John (Elijah) was in the Jordan baptising and announcing the arrival of Jesus the Messiah.

'Prepare the way for the Lord, make straight paths for him.'

**Mark 1:3**

## RESPOND
In what ways is the kingdom coming in your life? Perhaps you're missing it because it comes in unexpected ways. 'God, give me eyes to see you at work in the simple things of today.'

. . . . . . . . . . . . . . . . . . . . . . . . . . . . . . . . . . . . . . . . . . . . . . . . . . . . . . . . . . . . . . . . . .

**Bible in a year:** Isaiah 23,24;  Titus 3

# Wednesday 13 September

Mark 1:9–20

# Follow me

## PREPARE

As you come before the Lord today, ask him what he wants you to give to him... your worries, your fears, your time, your attention? Ask his Holy Spirit to lead you and empower you.

• • • • • • • • • • • • • • • • • • • • • • • • • • • • • • • • • • • • • • • • • • • • • • • •

## READ

**Mark 1:9–20**

## EXPLORE

As we read through the Gospel of Mark, it doesn't take long before we notice the extreme pace of events throughout the Gospel! One minute Jesus is being baptised and God is telling the world that his Son who he loves is here (vs 9–11); then, he's being tempted in the wilderness by Satan (vs 12,13); next, we hear John the Baptist has been imprisoned, and Jesus has taken up John's mantle of announcing the kingdom of God: 'The kingdom of God has come near' (vs 14,15).

Then, we see Jesus walking along the shoreline of the Sea of Galilee. He calls to Simon (Peter) and Andrew to follow him, and he will make them fishers, but this time, of people (v 17). Immediately they leave their family business and all they have ever known to follow Jesus. The three of them walk further down the shoreline and they see two more brothers, James and John. Again, Jesus calls, and again, they leave their family business and follow Jesus. Why? Because the kingdom of heaven has come near, is moving fast and they don't want to miss out on what's about to unfold.

'See, I am doing a new thing! Now it springs up; do you not perceive it? I am making a way in the wilderness and streams in the wasteland.'

**Isaiah 43:19**

## RESPOND

What might Jesus be asking you to let go of in your life, in order to follow him and see the kingdom of God break into your life in a new way?

• • • • • • • • • • • • • • • • • • • • • • • • • • • • • • • • • • • • • • • • • • • • • • • •

**Bible in a year:** Isaiah 25,26; Psalm 104

# The power of God

## PREPARE
In what way do you need to encounter the power of God in your life today? Take a moment to talk to God about that.

·······················································································

## READ
**Mark 1:21–34**

## EXPLORE
In 1 John 3:8 the writer says: 'The reason the Son of God appeared was to destroy the devil's work.' In today's reading we see this truth painted for us in full technicolour. While John, writing in his letter, was looking back at what transpired through the life, death and resurrection of Jesus, here Mark is giving us a snapshot of what Jesus is doing and will ultimately accomplish completely.

We see demonic forces, even in the house of God, in a man possessed by an unclean spirit (vs 23,24). This spirit recognises Jesus as 'the Holy One of God' and is powerless to withstand him. Next, Jesus goes to the house of Simon and Andrew and heals Simon's mother-in-law from her fever. Later, all the sick and possessed are coming to this home because word has got out that Jesus can heal and deliver (vs 32–34).

Mark paints for us a picture that God in Christ has come to his people once more. The demonic forces that cause sickness and death are powerless to stand against him and are going to be overthrown once and for all (v 24).

> The people brought to Jesus all who were ill and demon-possessed ... and Jesus healed many who had various diseases.

**Mark 1:32,34**

## RESPOND
Jesus came to free us from our sin, our suffering and the brokenness we experience in the world around us. Where have you seen this in your life to be true? Thank God for his goodness.

·······················································································

**Bible in a year:** Isaiah 27,28;  Philemon 1

## Friday 15 September
### Mark 1:35–45

# Living from rest

**PREPARE**

**What things are troubling you and weighing you down today? Ask the Lord to allow you to set them to one side as you enter into time with him now.**

**READ**

**Mark 1:35–45**

**EXPLORE**

According to some research it is thought that people today spend well over two hours a day on social media.* We are surrounded by constant demands for our attention, trying to divert us from what we should be focusing on.

In today's passage we see Jesus addressing the very real and pressing need to get away from distractions and from people's expectations of him, in order to spend time alone with his Father. In John 5:19 Jesus says that the Son only does 'what he sees his Father doing'. In order for that to happen, Jesus needs to spend time listening to the Father. As a result of this time alone with him, Jesus knows where he needs to go, where to share the gospel, and to whom he needs to minister (vs 39,42). He forgoes the expectations which people try to place on him (vs 36,37), and the busyness of his surroundings, and simply asks his Father what to do

next. And then, when he has heard, he simply obeys.

> Very early in the morning, while it was still dark, Jesus got up, left the house and went off to a solitary place, where he prayed.
>
> **Mark 1:35**

**RESPOND**

Ask the Lord to show you where you get side-tracked from his purposes. Invite the Holy Spirit to lead you where he wants you to be today. Are there any practical steps you might take to reduce distractions from his purposes in your life?

*https://tinyurl.com/ftw8x56d

**Bible in a year:** Isaiah 29,30;  Hebrews 1

# The lordship of Christ

## PREPARE
**What is the condition of your heart as you come to Jesus? Anxious, happy, peaceful, in pain? Invite his Holy Spirit to come and minister to you now.**

. . . . . . . . . . . . . . . . . . . . . . . . . . . . . . . . . . . . . . . . . . . . . . . . . . . . . . . . . . . . . . . . . . . . . . .

## READ
**Mark 2:1–12**

## EXPLORE

Up to this point in Jesus' ministry, he has been healing the sick and casting out demons. Remarkable acts – but not unheard of in first-century Jerusalem. Now, as Jesus stands over this paralysed man, everyone around him is watching, expectant of seeing his physical ailment healed. But Jesus identifies a sickness far deeper and in more urgent need of attention than his paralysis – namely, this man's spiritual sickness. Rather than first speaking words of physical healing, Jesus pronounces his sins as forgiven (v 5).

The teachers of the Law are incredulous because they know Jesus has just proclaimed himself as one with God (vs 6,7), which, if true, makes him Messiah. Everything they have built and lived for – their position, their status – is under threat. Jesus knows what they are thinking and challenges their hard and resistant hearts (v 9). As the man walks home, he is living and breathing evidence that Messiah has come. God's kingdom is breaking in to make a sin-sick world right once more, and to restore those who would receive Jesus as Lord back to the Father.

> '… the Son of Man has authority on earth to forgive sins.' So he said to the man, '… get up, take your mat and go home.' He got up … and walked out…
>
> **Mark 2:10–12**

## RESPOND
CS Lewis pointed out that you cannot say Jesus is a great moral teacher without acknowledging him as Lord.* Are there ways in which you accept Jesus as friend, healer, counsellor, but resist his lordship? Ask him to help you surrender those to him now.

*CS Lewis, *Mere Christianity*, Harper Collins

. . . . . . . . . . . . . . . . . . . . . . . . . . . . . . . . . . . . . . . . . . . . . . . . . . . . . . . . . . . . . . . . . . . . . . .

**Bible in a year:** Isaiah 31,32;  Psalm 105

## Sunday 17 September
Psalm 110

# Jesus – priest and king

## PREPARE
Writing about his vision of Jesus, John wrote: 'I saw heaven standing open and there before me was a white horse, whose rider is called Faithful and True' (Revelation 19:11). Come to him and worship him now.

. . . . . . . . . . . . . . . . . . . . . . . . . . . . . . . . . . . . . . . . . . . . . . . .

## READ
**Psalm 110**

## EXPLORE
How do you picture Jesus in your mind's eye? As the first-century Jewish rabbi who walked the streets of Nazareth and Galilee? That's a good place to start. But if that's *only* how we see Jesus, we will only have a limited picture. In this psalm David prophesies concerning Jesus the coming Messiah, and, just as a coin has two sides, here we see Jesus' two sides: he is both priest, who ministers between God and man (v 4); and also conquering king, who wages war against all who oppose him (vs 2,3,5,6).

We need a priest who can mediate between God and man and offer himself as the priestly sacrifice who atones for sin (1 John 2:1,2). But we also need a conquering king who will pursue evil and suffering, sin and death (Ephesians 6:12) until they are utterly destroyed and the rule and reign of his kingdom are established for ever.

Jesus is our great high priest (v 4), the Lord of lords and King of kings (v 2). He makes you right before God, and one day, he will reign victorious over sin and death (1 Corinthians 15:55).

The LORD says to my lord: 'Sit at my right hand until I make your enemies a footstool for your feet.'

**Psalm 110:1**

## RESPOND
Take a moment to read through Revelation 19 and reflect on the picture of Jesus you see there. 'Amen, Hallelujah!' (Revelation 19:4).

. . . . . . . . . . . . . . . . . . . . . . . . . . . . . . . . . . . . . . . . . . . . . . . .

**Bible in a year:** Isaiah 33,34;  Hebrews 2

# Healing sin-sick hearts

## PREPARE
Ask God to reveal to you today the truth of Jesus' work which has brought you into his kingdom.

· · · · · · · · · · · · · · · · · · · · · · · · · · · · · · · · · · · · · · · · · · · · · · · · ·

## READ
**Mark 2:13–22**

## EXPLORE
How did you come to follow Jesus? While everyone's story is beautiful and unique, ultimately, we all share the same story of salvation: Jesus saw us, he called us and we followed him (v 14).

Because Jesus operates in that way, as opposed to calling people to performance and strict moral observance, people who place their trust in their own moral performance and behaviour get nervous (v 18). They think that, rather than going to where Jesus is (v 16), he should come and be with them, because their performance has earned them that right. The pride in our hearts, just as in the Pharisees' in this passage, means we tend to judge ourselves as better than we are – and others as worse than we are.

But the moral standard for entry into the kingdom of God is not OK, good or even very good, but is, in fact, perfection.

The new wine of the kingdom is the law fulfilled in Jesus (v 22). It is no longer about our performance, but depends on Jesus. Because Jesus meets that standard, our entry is found only in and through him, the doorway to the kingdom of God (John 10:9).

'It is not the healthy who need a doctor, but those who are ill. I have not come to call the righteous, but sinners.'

**Mark 2:17**

## RESPOND
In what ways do you place hope in your ability to impress God? Ask God to free you from the slavery of moral performance, and to help you see Jesus alone as enough.

· · · · · · · · · · · · · · · · · · · · · · · · · · · · · · · · · · · · · · · · · · · · · · · · ·

**Bible in a year:** Isaiah 35,36;  Hebrews 3

## Tuesday 19 September
Mark 2:23–28

# A foretaste of eternity

### PREPARE
What is on your to-do list today? As you come to God now, ask him to help you to lay those things down, so you can rest in his goodness while you focus on him.

· · · · · · · · · · · · · · · · · · · · · · · · · · · · · · · · · · · · · · · · · · · · · · · · · · · · · · · · · · · · ·

### READ
**Mark 2:23–28**

### EXPLORE
When you think of the term 'Sabbath', what comes to mind? Maybe things like shops being closed on Sunday, going to church, resting, rules...

The people at the time of Jesus had forgotten that God had given the Sabbath as a day of rest to humanity (v 27), as a reminder that God the Creator is in control of all things (Genesis 2:2,3). He is the source of our provision and rest, and it is important for us to be able to exist beyond and outside of our labour (Exodus 20:8–11). Abraham Joshua Heschel wrote: 'Unless one learns how to relish the taste of Sabbath ... one will be unable to enjoy the taste of eternity in the world to come.'*

Jesus is King of his kingdom and is Lord of the Sabbath (v 28). When we participate in Sabbath, we switch out of 'work mode' and get to enjoy God's good gifts to us. And, as we get a foretaste of what life eternal in the kingdom is like, we 'taste and see that the LORD is good' (Psalm 34:8).

> 'The Sabbath was made for man, not man for the Sabbath.'
>
> **Mark 2:27**

---

### RESPOND
When was the last time you took a 'proper' Sabbath – turned off the phone and emails, spent time with loved ones doing what brings you joy (cooking, reading, films, walks, DIY...)? Try it!

---

*Abraham Joshua Heschel, *The Sabbath*, 1951

· · · · · · · · · · · · · · · · · · · · · · · · · · · · · · · · · · · · · · · · · · · · · · · · · · · · · · · · · · · · ·

**Bible in a year:** Isaiah 37,38;  Hebrews 4

# Good over evil

## PREPARE

What do you need from God today? Ask him, knowing that he is your Father who loves to give good gifts to his children (Luke 11:13).

. . . . . . . . . . . . . . . . . . . . . . . . . . . . . . . . . . . . . . . . . . . . . . . . . . . . . . . . . . . . . . . . . . . .

## READ

**Mark 3:1–6**

## EXPLORE

I'm allergic to wasp stings. If I get stung, I need an EpiPen injection quickly or the consequences could be fatal. Imagine if I came barging into your house, begging you for an EpiPen, asking you to call an ambulance because I'd just been stung – and then you refused because, in your house, if you don't knock politely and wait, you don't get what you want!

It sounds absurd, doesn't it? My assumption is that most people wouldn't do that, yet that is what the Pharisees did every day with their man-made rules (v 2). By preferring their customs to what the kingdom of God was doing in and through Jesus, they withheld good from people for the sake of their tradition.

The kingdom of God is no respecter of tradition and human order because God is always reaching out to people, and they are more important to him than traditions and customs (v 5). The kingdom of God has come in Jesus, and nothing is going to stop it, not even well-intentioned propriety and customs.

> Then Jesus asked them, 'Which is lawful on the Sabbath: to do good or to do evil, to save life or to kill?' But they remained silent.
>
> **Mark 3:4**

## RESPOND

We are called to bring the good news of Jesus to the world around us. In prayer, ask God to show you if there are any places in your heart where religious tradition has become more important than obeying the Holy Spirit.

. . . . . . . . . . . . . . . . . . . . . . . . . . . . . . . . . . . . . . . . . . . . . . . . . . . . . . . . . . . . . . . . . . . .

**Bible in a year:** Isaiah 39,40;  Psalm 106

# Thursday 21 September
Mark 3:7–19

# Underdogs not top dogs

## PREPARE

'The Lord does not look at the things people look at. People look at the outward appearance, but the Lord looks at the heart' (1 Samuel 16:7). As you turn to God now, what does he see in your heart?

......................................................................

## READ
**Mark 3:7–19**

## EXPLORE

To be a part of this kingdom of God that Jesus is announcing and is breaking into this world, as we have seen, it is not enough to passively observe tradition and rules. The kingdom of God demands action from us which is simply this – to follow Jesus (1:17,18).

Jesus doesn't pick his team the way we might, however. Have you ever assembled a team for a project? You probably look for the brightest, the most competent, the best at following instructions and the team players. Not Jesus! He chooses traitors to Israel (Matthew the tax collector), xenophobes (Bartholomew, aka Nathanael*), political activists (Simon the Zealot), doubters (Thomas), deniers (Peter), hotheads (James and John) and even betrayers (Judas).

Thank God that Jesus doesn't choose the brightest and best! The only qualification seems to be a willingness to follow him wherever he goes. In his kingdom, Jesus doesn't assemble crack squads to storm the enemy; he simply invites anyone, even the most unqualified, on the adventure of following him. Will you follow him today?

> Jesus went up on a mountainside and called to him those he wanted, and they came to him.
>
> **Mark 3:13**

## RESPOND

What has Jesus been asking you to do recently? Have you done it? Ask Jesus as you come to him today to help you to trust him and obey what he's asking you to do.

*See John 1:43–50. Bartholomew and Nathanael are probably the same person

......................................................................

**Bible in a year:** Isaiah 41,42;  Hebrews 5

# God's big global family

## PREPARE
Ask God to speak clearly through his Holy Spirit so you can hear how he wants you to follow Jesus today.

..................................................................................................

## READ
**Mark 3:20–35**

## EXPLORE
Unmet expectations are one of the biggest causes of friction in relationships, whether spousal, familial, work-related or friendships. When Jesus comes on the scene, he shatters the religious leaders' expectations of who Messiah is and how he operates, to the point that they say he is demon possessed (v 22). Many Christians worry whether they have committed an unforgivable sin (v 29) but in verse 30 Jesus is clear that the sin he's referring to is that of accusing him of having an evil spirit. Someone who is worrying about that is highly unlikely to have committed that sin!

His family, however genuine their intentions towards him were, had to deal with the fact that Jesus came for *all* people, and for him there is no special privilege for blood relatives (vs 33–35). Yes, he loves and honours his parents and loves his brothers, but they are no more worthy of the kingdom than anyone else. Paradoxically, he would give his own flesh and blood to redeem the world (including his earthly family).

One of the great mysteries of God's kingdom is that God became flesh and was born to a human family. Now in Christ he makes a way for all humanity to be adopted into his global family.

'Whoever does God's will is my brother and sister and mother.'
**Mark 3:35**

---

## RESPOND
Ask God to show you anywhere in your heart where you feel more, or less, deserving than others of God's grace. Ask him to replace that lie with his truth.

---

..................................................................................................

**Bible in a year:** Isaiah 43,44;  Hebrews 6

## Saturday 23 September
Mark 4:1–20

# 'Change my heart, O God'

## PREPARE
As you prepare to come to God, confess your sin to him, knowing that he loves you, forgives you, wipes your slate clean and washes you whiter than snow (Psalm 51:7).

....................................................

## READ
**Mark 4:1–20**

## EXPLORE
In one of Jesus' most famous parables explaining what the kingdom of God is like, he tells his disciples what his parables are about: namely, making known what has up to this point been kept secret about the kingdom of God (v 11).

He explains to the disciples – who still don't understand (which probably means we wouldn't either!) – that the kingdom of God works like this. The Father (the sower) has sown the Word (Jesus) on to all kinds of ground (humanity). And most of the ground is resistant to Jesus for various reasons.

Fruitfulness in the kingdom then simply comes from having hearts that gladly and humbly receive Jesus and choose to follow him. They allow him to work in them by the power of the Holy Spirit, turning them from being hard as *stone* into how they were always created to be – as *flesh* (Ezekiel 36:26). I don't know

about you, but my heart can quickly become a hard and rocky ground, and the weeds of pride get in there. I need the Holy Spirit to water and work on me every day.

'Others, like seed sown on good soil, hear the word, accept it, and produce a crop – some thirty, some sixty, some a hundred times what was sown.'

**Mark 4:20**

---

## RESPOND
Ask God to reveal to you the condition of the soil of your heart. Is it hard? Shallow? Full of weeds and distraction? Fruitful? Ask him to work in you through the power of his Spirit.

---

....................................................

**Bible in a year:** Isaiah 45,46;  Psalm 107

# Wisdom in a foolish world

## PREPARE
On this Sunday, come before the Lord with your uncertainty and fears. Ask him to give you wisdom for the way ahead.

. . . . . . . . . . . . . . . . . . . . . . . . . . . . . . . . . . . . . . . . . . . . . . . . . . . . . . . . . . . . . . . . . . . . . . . . . . . . . . . . . . . . . .

## READ
**Psalm 111**

## EXPLORE
Jesus asked, 'Can the blind lead the blind? Will they not both fall into a pit?' (Luke 6:39). Whether it's agony aunts, social media, political commentators or star signs, we are bombarded with people who want to tell us how we should think about things and how we should respond to various situations. We live in a world full of blind guides and we need wisdom.

In this psalm the writer is singing with great joy about how he loves the works and precepts of the Lord (v 7), and about how wisdom begins when we have a right view of God. He is gracious and compassionate (v 4), righteous (v 3), faithful and just (v 7), holy and awesome (v 9).

When we see God's laws not as arbitrary but as given by a holy and good God, who loves us and leads us into life and flourishing, then we take delight in knowing his law – and knowing him. As we do so, we stand at the beginning of wisdom, and the scales fall from our eyes. We are no longer blind, but able to see clearly – we can also lead others with us into the wisdom that is ultimately found in Jesus (Proverbs 8:22–32).

The fear of the LORD is the beginning of wisdom.

**Psalm 111:10**

## RESPOND
Where do I seek wisdom? Ask God if there are some things to which you need to pay less attention. Ask his help to seek his wisdom more.

. . . . . . . . . . . . . . . . . . . . . . . . . . . . . . . . . . . . . . . . . . . . . . . . . . . . . . . . . . . . . . . . . . . . . . . . . . . . . . . . . . . . . .

**Bible in a year:** Isaiah 47,48;  Hebrews 7

# Monday 25 September
Mark 4:21-25

# His kingdom is coming!

## PREPARE
**As you come to the Lord through his Word, ask him to lift your eyes to see a wider perspective of what he is doing – in your life and in the world around you.**

. . . . . . . . . . . . . . . . . . . . . . . . . . . . . . . . . . . . . . . . . . . . . . . . . . . . . . . . . . . .

## READ
**Mark 4:21-25**

## EXPLORE
In a song by Bruce Cockburn,* there's a line that says: 'Gotta kick at the darkness 'til it bleeds daylight.' So, we might say, it is with the kingdom of God.

As we see, all through Mark's Gospel, the kingdom of God is kicking against the darkness of sin, of indifference, of religious and spiritual opposition and hostility, and the cracks are beginning to show: 'Whatever is hidden is meant to be disclosed' (v 22). And the promise of this kingdom is that it's never going to stop until the whole world is lit up with the glory of the Lord (Revelation 21:23; Habakkuk 2:14).

Do you long for that? When sin and death are no more? When justice and righteousness reign? When there are no more tears and no more pain, when everything is under the rule and reign of Jesus, the Prince of Peace? If not, the truth is that those people who try to hold on to their lives will lose them (Matthew 16:25), but if you *do* long for that day then you will be satisfied more than you could ever imagine (v 25).

> 'Whoever has will be given more; whoever does not have, even what they have will be taken from them.'
>
> **Mark 4:25**

## RESPOND
Are you aware of areas in your life where you are resistant to God's rule and reign? Is there persistent sin, pride or wanting to keep control over some areas of your life? Bring these to God now.

*'Lovers in a Dangerous Time', 1984

. . . . . . . . . . . . . . . . . . . . . . . . . . . . . . . . . . . . . . . . . . . . . . . . . . . . . . . . . . . .

**Bible in a year:** Isaiah 49,50;  Hebrews 8

# Nothing will stop it!

## PREPARE

'Are we weak and heavy-laden, cumbered with a load of care? Precious Saviour, still our refuge. Take it to the Lord in prayer...'* Do that now.

........................................................................

## READ

**Mark 4:26–34**

## EXPLORE

Charles Spurgeon (1834–1892) apparently said, 'When you go through a trial, the sovereignty of God is the pillow upon which you lay your head', and the Puritans used to say something similar: 'Providence is a soft pillow for anxious heads.'** Sometimes in life we might feel like everything is going well, there is no stress, we feel close to the Lord and all is right in our world. But such times are usually fleeting and rare. Usually, all of us have a mixture of things going on.

In these parables of the kingdom, there is reassurance. In good times or bad, the kingdom of God is at work in the world, and also in us (v 27). It has taken root; it is growing like a seed and it won't stop (vs 31,32). Our sin can't stop it; our good deeds can't enhance it. Sometimes this growth feels good, sometimes it feels painful, but at all times we can know and trust that '... he who began a good work in you will carry it on to completion until the day of Christ Jesus' (Philippians 1:6).

'Night and day, whether he sleeps or gets up, the seed sprouts and grows, though he does not know how.'

**Mark 4:27**

> ## RESPOND
> Ask the Lord to reveal to you how he is working in your life in the good, and even in the hard things, to form you into the likeness of Jesus. And ask him for grace to keep going.

*Joseph Scriven, 'What a Friend We Have in Jesus', 1855
**Charles Spurgeon, *The Treasury of David*, 1869

........................................................................

**Bible in a year:** Isaiah 51,52; Hebrews 9

# Wednesday 27 September
Mark 4:35–41

# Trust and obey

## PREPARE
As you come to Jesus, ask him to give you peace about the things that are troubling you and might distract you now (Philippians 4:6,7).

• • • • • • • • • • • • • • • • • • • • • • • • • • • • • • • • • • • • • • • • • • • • • •

## READ
**Mark 4:35–41**

## EXPLORE
All through our readings from Mark's Gospel we have seen Jesus doing incredible things: healing people (2:1–12), casting out demons (1:21–28) and asserting himself as Lord over religious observance (2:23–28). Now, in a climactic hinge point in Mark's Gospel, we see Jesus leading the disciples into the middle of the sea of Galilee, knowing that he is leading them into a storm (v 35).

How do you respond to a Jesus who leads his followers into storms? The answer to that question is the focus of these verses (vs 40,41). These disciples, who had seen Jesus doing amazing things, still hadn't understood the message that the kingdom of God is breaking into the world – 'Who is this? Even the wind and the waves obey him' (v 41) – and nothing is going to stop it: not Jesus being asleep and not actively present with them (v 38); not even a

storm that terrifies these hardened fishermen (v 40).

Jesus would ask us today, and every day, whether we trust him even when the odds are stacked against us. Jesus calls us not to be followers who understand, but followers who simply trust and obey.

> He said to his disciples, 'Why are you so afraid? Do you still have no faith?'
>
> **Mark 4:40**

## RESPOND
What do you find easiest about following Jesus? What do you find difficult? Thank him for those things which you love to do. Ask him to give you grace and humility in those which you find difficult.

• • • • • • • • • • • • • • • • • • • • • • • • • • • • • • • • • • • • • • • • • • • • • •

**Bible in a year:** Isaiah 53,54;  Psalms 108,109

# It's your turn now!

**About the writer**
**Alison Allen**

After 14 years of being involved in mission in and from Romania, Alison returned to the UK in 2014 and now lives in Suffolk with her husband, two young children and three cats. Alison is currently working in the local Public Health department, whilst researching millennials in international mission for a PhD.

Have you ever taken over a job from someone else? In practice it often doesn't go very well! In theory, however, you will watch your predecessor doing the job, learn from him or her and build relationships with those you are going to work with. As you step into the role, you will seek to achieve a balance between continuity and making the role your own.

In 1 Kings 19 we read how God sends Elijah to anoint Elisha as his successor. Elisha accepts the invitation and goes with him, becoming his assistant. Between 1 Kings 19 and 2 Kings 2 there is a clearly intentional period of discipleship and mentoring: Elisha serves Elijah and assists him for a number of years. When Elijah is taken up to heaven, Elisha is ready to step straight into the role, acting and speaking with confidence. The other prophets watch Elisha pick up Elijah's cloak and very quickly recognise him as Elijah's successor, although some insist on going to look for Elijah. Elisha's spiritual authority is immediately displayed as he parts the Jordan (2 Kings 2:14) and then proceeds to perform the miracles we will read about over the next two weeks.

Though not a perfect parallel, there are lessons for us as disciples of our Master, Jesus. We walk with him and observe what he does, and also receive his Spirit so that we may continue to do his works (John 14:12–17; Acts 1:8).

# Sources of knowledge

**PREPARE**

'Abba! Father!' What does it mean to you that we can call God 'Father'?

∙∙∙∙∙∙∙∙∙∙∙∙∙∙∙∙∙∙∙∙∙∙∙∙∙∙∙∙∙∙∙∙∙∙∙∙∙∙∙∙∙∙∙∙∙∙∙∙∙∙∙∙∙∙

**READ**

**2 Kings 1:1–18**

**EXPLORE**

Besides falling from a window, King Ahaziah makes two big mistakes in this passage: he seeks a word from the wrong god and then he tries to tell the man of God what to do. It's pretty obvious in Ahaziah's story that these were bad choices, but I wonder how often we're tempted to do something similar?

Maybe I don't send messengers to a foreign temple, but when I need to make a decision or consider the consequences of my actions, where do I turn? Do I search the Scriptures and seek to discern the will of God? Or do I listen to the voices, judgements and priorities of the world? If, like Ahaziah, I don't like the answer the Lord gives me, do I try to force God to do what I want? The captain who succeeded in persuading Elijah to come was the one who approached humbly and fearing God (vs 13–15).

This story is especially tragic because twice (in verses 4 and 16b) Elijah appears to tie Ahaziah's fate to his seeking a god who is not the Lord. Idolatry really matters to God: he is jealous for his people. Let us take care to seek his Word and his will and not be tempted away by the shining idols we see worshipped by those around us.

> 'Is it because there is no God in Israel that you are going off to consult Baal-Zebub, the god of Ekron?'
>
> **2 Kings 1:3**

**RESPOND**

Ask the Lord to show you if there are ways in which you have been listening to the wrong voices.

∙∙∙∙∙∙∙∙∙∙∙∙∙∙∙∙∙∙∙∙∙∙∙∙∙∙∙∙∙∙∙∙∙∙∙∙∙∙∙∙∙∙∙∙∙∙∙∙∙∙∙∙∙∙

**Bible in a year:** Isaiah 55,56;  Hebrews 10

# Passing the baton

## PREPARE
**Pray for Christian leaders you know, that they will walk with God and serve him faithfully.**

.................................................................

## READ
**2 Kings 2:1–25**

## EXPLORE
Although Elijah had been commanded by God to anoint Elisha as his successor (1 Kings 19:16–21), he seems determined to get rid of him on this final journey. Three times (vs 2,4,6) he gives Elisha the opportunity to stay behind. Elijah knew first-hand the cost of being the chief prophet: he knew that it would not be easy for Elisha to pick up his cloak and his calling. Three times Elisha insists on staying faithful.

When Elisha requests a 'double portion' of Elijah's spirit (v 9), he isn't saying that he wants to be greater than Elijah: he is asking to be considered Elijah's first son. Traditionally, the first-born son would receive a double portion of the father's inheritance (Deuteronomy 21:17). When Elisha was first called, he literally burned his former life (1 Kings 19:21) in order to become Elijah's assistant. In today's passage he reasserts this whole-hearted commitment.

Elisha then demonstrates his new God-given authority by preserving life (vs 19–22) and taking life (vs 23–25). In approaching Elisha (v 19), the people of the city were seeking God. The youths (v 23), on the other hand, rejected God when they rejected Elisha.

And he replied, 'As surely as the LORD lives and as you live, I will not leave you.' So the two of them walked on.

**2 Kings 2:6**

> **RESPOND:**
> Read John 21:15–17 and imagine yourself in Peter's place, having that conversation with Jesus.

.................................................................

**Bible in a year:** Isaiah 57,58;  Hebrews 11

## Saturday 30 September
2 Kings 3:1–27

# Who calls the shots?

**Still your heart and mind before God. Note down and put aside for later any thoughts that might distract you.**

. . . . . . . . . . . . . . . . . . . . . . . . . . . . . . . . . . . . . . . . . . . . . . . . . . . . . . . . . . . . . . . . . . . . . . . . . . . . .

### READ
**2 Kings 3:1–27**

### EXPLORE

Verse 2 tells us that King Joram was not a good king, but neither was he as bad as the previous generation. Although he removed the 'stone of Baal' (v 2), Joram continued in the 'sins of Jeroboam' (v 3) which were the worship of other gods.

Although King Joram twice asserts that the Lord has brought the armies together in a desert to die (vs 10,13), there is no mention of the Lord's involvement in the decision of the three kings to go to war against Moab. Despite his general lack of respect for the Lord, Joram views Moab's rebellion against Israel as an affront against the Lord and the war on Moab, therefore, as God's battle. So King Joram of Israel blames the Lord when the armies find themselves in a place without water (v 10). However, King Jehoshaphat of Judah suggests finding a prophet of the Lord to ask for guidance (v 11). Joram is ready to blame the Lord for his problems, but doesn't think to seek him for a solution. Happily though, he goes along with the plan to consult Elisha.

People are often quick to blame God when things go wrong, but slow to seek him for guidance either before embarking on a course of action or when it all goes pear-shaped. Let's be those who seek the Lord at every step.

> But Jehoshaphat asked, 'Is there no prophet of the LORD here, through whom we may enquire of the LORD?'
>
> **2 Kings 3:11**

---

### RESPOND
Ask the Lord for fresh guidance in your current circumstances.

---

. . . . . . . . . . . . . . . . . . . . . . . . . . . . . . . . . . . . . . . . . . . . . . . . . . . . . . . . . . . . . . . . . . . . . . . . . . . . .

**Bible in a year:** Isaiah 59,60; Psalms 110,111